the
Mommy
Manual

responsible
Patience
Gentleness/Spirit
nurturing
loyal
Generous
independent
obience to god
Curiousity/god
loving
Compassionate
brave believers
Courage
Optimism
Wisdom
Gratitude

the Mommy Manual

Planting Roots That Give Your Children Wings

Barbara Curtis

Revell
Grand Rapids, Michigan

Published by Fleming H. Revell
a division of Baker Publishing Group
P.O. Box 6287, Grand Rapids, MI 49516-6287

Printed in the United States of America

Library of Congress Cataloging-in-Publication Data
Curtis, Barbara, 1948–
    The mommy manual : planting roots that give your children wings / Barbara Curtis.
        p.   cm.
    ISBN 0-8007-5982-6 (pbk.)
    1. Motherhood—Religious aspects—Christianity. 2. Parenting—Religious aspects—Christianity. 3. Mothers—Religious life. I. Title.
BV4529.18C88 2005
248.8′431—dc22   2004030786

Thank you to my family:
Tripp, who started it all;
Samantha and Kip, and grandchildren Tim, Patrick, Andrew,
Jeffrey, and Trinity;
Jasmine and Nathan, and grandchildren Gabriella, Christian,
Kaitlyn, and Elizabeth;
Joshua, Matt, Ben, and Zach,
Sophia and Madeleine,
Jonny, Jesse, Daniel, and Justin

Contents

Contents

Preface

Hooray for mommies!

Hooray for mommies who get up every morning to hours filled with peanut butter and jelly, nursery rhymes, *The Wiggles*, skinned knees, wet beds, hurt feelings, groceries, tangled hair, Little League, play dates, car pools, music lessons, dentist visits, and perhaps—if you're blessed to be at that particular stage of motherhood—the unmistakable aroma of baby spit-up on your shoulder.

And hooray for mommies who face the usual daily dilemmas too: Do I have time to take a shower before *Dora the Explorer* is over? Does Jesse really need to see the doctor or will she examine him and say it's just a virus, leaving me feeling like we've wasted the morning? Is there anything I can throw together for dinner so I can put off the grocery store another day?

And through all the mommy moments, that still, small voice urges you to keep the washer and dryer going . . . 'cause if you don't, you and I both know there's no way you'll ever catch up. Just your basic everyday mommy routine, seasoned here and there with the unexpected: trips to the emergency room, plumbing problems, snow days, earthquakes, random haircuts (as in, one of your kids cuts the other's hair), unanticipated mural creation (your three-year-old decides the hallway lacks that certain something), and a vast array of other kid surprises.

(Did I mention the day my then two-year-old son Ben, who loved to watch Daddy water the grass in the evening, decided to help us out by watering the green carpet with the garden hose? Imagine how much that week—filled with rolled-back soggy carpets and turbo fans—set me back in whatever progress I had been trying to make.)

And isn't that one of the frustrating things about being a mommy?

We live in a world where success is measured by progress, as recorded on report cards, sales reports, performance reviews, and pay raises, and symbolized by ribbons, trophies, and merit badges. In our familes' lifetime, our husbands and our children will bring scores of these items home and make us proud. We'll put them in scrapbooks, sew them on uniforms, frame and hang them up for all to see.

But I don't know of any special award just for being a mom.

So for a moment, step back from the whirlwind of stuff families are made of. Stop for five minutes. Take a deep breath. Take a fresh look.

Imagine the turn-of-the-century carousel at the San Francisco Zoo, where my children rode colorfully crafted ponies, fantastic lions, and elegant ostriches while their dad and I faithfully smiled and waved as each one passed by.

How did it happen that the expression "I feel like I'm on a merry-go-round" came to mean something negative?

Imagine the children whirling round with smiles and laughter as their fantastic animals glide up and down.

Merry-go-rounds are fun!

Hold on to that thought the next time you feel overwhelmed and underappreciated or restless with the routine of being a mother.

Yes, our lives sometimes seem like the same old thing every day. Sometimes it seems we're not really getting anywhere. Sometimes we wonder what it's all about.

But what if we looked at it differently? What if we saw ourselves on that merry-go-round, gliding gracefully up and down in time to the sweet, old-fashioned carousel music? What if we could smile and laugh at the wonderful ride we've chosen? What if, instead of feeling frazzled, we felt excited and eager to see the smile of our heavenly Father each time we went around?

God is smiling at us, you know. He appreciates the job mommies do. Jesus said, "Whoever welcomes one of these little children in my name welcomes me; and whoever welcomes me does not welcome me but the one who sent me" (Mark 9:37).

You can count on it that God knows a mommy's job is difficult, that it requires self-sacrifice and receives little recognition. He knows a mommy's ups and downs, weaknesses and strengths.

Most of all he cares for mommies like you can't imagine.

Picture the parents watching their children on that San Francisco carousel—it's like God being there to give mommies some ooomph to the ride. Mommies only need remember to keep looking for him with each turn of that merry-go-round of motherhood.

In my motherhood-testing moments I remind myself to think of that merry-go-round I know on the boardwalk in Santa Cruz. It's old and not quite as grand as its cousin to the north, but it has something else that makes it special—brass rings. The rings come down a chute just far enough away so that the riders can hold on tight to the horse's pole with one hand while reaching out with the other. It's pretty easy for anyone over seven to reach the rings; and fun as it was just to grab a ring and throw it in the big clown mouth nearby, the ultimate goal was to grab the special brass ring. When someone grabbed that one, you'd hear a squeal of delight.

Now I have a picture for the expression "catching the brass ring."

That is just like another facet of the merry-go-round of motherhood. Besides looking to your heavenly Father for encouragement, you can also be reaching for the brass ring—that special moment when you know you've done your best and really gotten something priceless in return.

Some of that has to do with your choice to look for and find the joy in motherhood—new ways of perceiving your calling (because motherhood is sooooo much more than a job, after all).

And some of it has to do with understanding more about your children and the potentials God has built into their lives, then learning how to help them realize those potentials.

This is what *The Mommy Manual* is all about.

As a mommy who's been there, done that, and who after thirty-five years and twelve kids, plus nine grandchildren, is still being here and doing it, I know one thing for sure: being a mommy and helping your children realize their potential is the best way for you to realize your own.

Barbara Curtis
Waterford, Virginia
August 2004

Planting Roots
and Growing Wings

> Every good and perfect gift is from above, coming
> down from the Father of the heavenly lights, who
> does not change like shifting shadows.
>
> James 1:17

One of the greatest gifts I ever received was a nest of sparrows. I call it a gift because I know that when something good comes into our lives, it isn't just random but something meant just for us.

The nest of sparrows was a perfect gift for a mommy, so I knew God had to be involved. How else to explain why a pair of sparrows would set up shop in a corner of our patio right next to a busy sliding-glass door? Yes, when they started to build, we put a stop to using that door, but for months Tripp and I and all the kids, plus assorted friends, walked back and forth through the hallway inside, separated by only a layer of glass from our newest neighbors.

Not to mention the daily ruckus outside in the swimming pool. Or the weekly Moms' Day Out, where moms chattered on the sidelines while dozens of kids romped like otters in the pool for hours. Even just the Curtis kids, including four-in-a-row rowdy boys, couldn't keep the volume down.

So when I say ruckus, I mean ruckus.

Day after day, the sparrows seemed oblivious to our human commotion. Filled with purpose, they flew forth, returning faithfully with twigs, dry grass, and wisps of wool picked from a nearby field where our sheep grazed.

They built their nest on a light fixture hanging on the wall at right angles to the glass. We couldn't have asked for a better view. And yet, no matter how often we peered through the glass to observe their progress, and no matter how many guests we brought to watch with us, the sparrows went about their business as if nothing else in the world mattered.

And so for a few weeks, their lives became part of ours. We saw the mother lay her first egg, get up and look at it, and nestle her body over it. The next day she laid another egg. And so on until there were five.

Then we watched her sit, except for brief periods when the father would come to relieve her, practically shoving her out when she seemed reluctant to go. She would leave only to forage for her own food while he sat on the eggs.

We were thrilled the morning the first baby pushed its way out of its shell. Between lunch and laundry, we kept watch until dinnertime, when the last baby made its way safely through the process.

What a ruckus their little family made! What a comical picture the nest became, crowded with five teeny, scraggly bodies somehow supporting way-wide-open beaks clamoring for "Food! More food!" as Mommy and Daddy flew tirelessly back and forth with assorted morsels to drop into their greedy, screeching little mouths.

Each time the mom and dad drew near to the nest, the baby birds would pump up the volume, each vying to be the one chosen for the drop. I felt a tug of sympathy, as when I'm surrounded by four or five of my kids all clamoring at once, each trying to talk over the uproar. Isn't it wonderful being a mommy and so in demand?

Sometimes I wondered how the sparrow parents kept themselves going, as feeding their little flock took every minute of every day. Did they grab a morsel for themselves before picking up the one to bring home?

After all, when we say someone "eats like a bird" we're trying to say they don't eat very much. But that's not how it is at all. When the kids and I looked it up, we found that most birds eat half their body weight each day—and hummingbirds beat them all by eating twice their weight. Which means if one of us decided to eat like a bird, we'd be ordering a thousand or so Big Macs each day.

So if the mommy and daddy had not only themselves to feed but also those five little noisy mouths—plus with the babies needing extra food to grow and the parents needing extra food for working so hard—well, it's mind-boggling to contemplate the level of commitment bird-parenting requires.

But then, it's such a short time for them.

Birds grow fast, from pink, helpless little blind things to fledglings (a Middle English word that meant "ready to fly") mature enough to fly away to build their own nests, in only a matter of a few weeks.

Which brings up a big question for me about why we are the way we are. Why is it exactly that humans take so long to mature? Birds are a different classification, so three weeks to maturity doesn't seem outlandish. But even among mammals, why is it that foals and calves and lambs stand up and walk within minutes of birth, while our own infants take months to even sit upright without help, and almost a year, maybe more, to walk? Why, throughout the animal kingdom, are the young helpless only briefly, while our children need us for so long?

I guess I've been thinking about this ever since I started being a mom. And I've realized that what makes the difference is this: among other species, development is governed by instinct. The mother and father birds feed their babies because they have to, according to the instincts with which God created them. The baby birds grow and do what they're supposed to because they too are governed by instincts.

Not so with human mommies and daddies and the new lives we create. We don't have many instincts—I can think only of things that have to do with survival, like babies crying for food when they're hungry or people jerking their hand away from something that's hot.

What we have instead of instincts are potentials, given to us by God, which are best released when we are brought up in loving families.

God must have had something in mind when he created us this way—to be dependent on our families for a long time.

And after being a mother for thirty-five years, and being blessed to be best friends with my grown-up children while still raising seven at home, I've come to believe that God made it take so long to grow up for the sake of intimacy—so we could bond and love each other more. He did it so we could build strong relationships with each other.

We are made in God's image, and God made us to have relationship with him. As parents, we teach our children about relationship—from the moment we first respond to meeting their needs for food and warmth and comfort to the time when they are ready to leave the nest to begin a relationship with the world on their own.

God also built some wonderful potentials into children, potentials that will help them grow to be joyful, gracious, caring, and compassionate people. But these potentials are best nurtured and encouraged in the earliest years—well before you send your child off to school or begin to teach him yourself. Later there may be teachers, coaches, mentors in your child's life. But you will always be your child's primary teacher—and the things you teach in the early years are far more important than quadratic equations.

Just in case that sounds a little scary or intimidating, keep this in mind: God doesn't call the equipped, he equips the called. You were called to be a mommy, and on-the-job training is provided pretty much 24/7. The lessons never stop. Sometimes when I look back over my motherhood, I'm not sure who learned more, my kids or me.

God is always revealing to us more about who we are, so we can become better mothers. As a mommy, I've been so surprised every time I've encountered some self-imposed limitation or inability to think outside the box. And I've been challenged to grow and change. Actually, if this were a fair world, many mommies who'd served their families well would be wearing medals of honor.

It's a big responsibility being a mommy. But the bottom line is this: you can count on God to provide for you every step of the way—not just through major catastrophes but in the daily grind and through all the tears and triumphs. You can find him in the smallest moments of the day—even as you push your toddler on the swing or change a diaper or kiss your baby good night.

17

A mommy bird feeds her babies until they are ready to go out on their own. We have so much more to do. And right up there near the top of the list is helping our children discover who they are—not just the God-given potentials we all share but the unique set of gifts he has given each one to accomplish the plan he has for their lives.

That's what *The Mommy Manual* is all about. In this book, I hope to give you:

- the keys to unlock your child's potential
- ways to tune in to your child's unique gifts
- secrets of joyful parenting
- encouragement for your journey

Okay, so I know motherhood is filled with runny noses and muddy floors and refrigerators that empty too fast. I know some days my minivan's runnin' on empty and, honey, so am I. That's when the inspiration we glean from the things we read comes in handy.

Don't just save what you read and file it away in the Barbara Curtis file. Keep it on your mental desktop as much as you can. Think of it when your son is wiping a runny nose on his shirt sleeve or your daughter is whining about the weather or the baby has spit up on your shoulder as you're out the door for a Bible study.

Close your eyes. Take a deep breath. And another. Now open your eyes and try to see your imperfect children the way God sees them—each as a remarkable bundle of possibilities, with many of those possibilities dependent on you for release. At times like that, I also try to think of myself the way God sees me—with my own balking, whining, and other far-from-wonderful behaviors.

Knowing how much God loves me in spite of my own inconsistencies and failures—uh, I mean, opportunities for growth—how can I do anything other than try my best to pass on that unconditional and everlasting love to my kids? When I think of myself as God's child and remember how patient he's been with me, it makes it so much easier to be patient with almost anything my children come up with.

Besides, by the time you finish reading this book, you'll know many things about your children that will make the going so much better.

The thing is, there's so much more to being a human than there is to being a bird . . . which isn't to say birds aren't wonderfully important. I think of that 1905 hymn "His Eye Is on the Sparrow"—a simple, old-timey hymn I first heard warbled by somebody's great-grandmother at a luncheon honoring Elisabeth Elliot. Although the soloist's voice had obviously lost some oomph with the passing of so many years, the sweet power of the lyrics had me hanging on each word. The simple melody is one of those things that has blessed me when some mothering days demand more than I feel I can handle. I love the second verse and the refrain.

"Let not your heart be troubled," His tender word I hear,
And resting on His goodness, I lose my doubts and fears;
Though by the path He leadeth, but one step I may see;
His eye is on the sparrow, and I know He watches me;
His eye is on the sparrow, and I know He watches me.
I sing because I'm happy,
I sing because I'm free,
For His eye is on the sparrow,
And I know He watches me.

The Ultimate Hymnal!

Find the lyrics and melody—plus pictures, Scripture, and stories—for any hymn or gospel song (well, at least 4,600 of them!) at www.cyberhymnal.org. Here's a real reason to spend oodles of time in front of the computer, singing along with your kids!

The hymn is based on Luke 12:6–7: "Are not five sparrows sold for two pennies? Yet not one of them is forgotten by God. Indeed, the very hairs of your head are all numbered. Don't be afraid; you are worth more than many sparrows."

I think birds are one of the most marvelous of God's creations. When our family goes to the zoo, we oooh and aaah at the flamingoes and parrots and ostriches. At home in Virginia, I oooh and aaah at the color flash of the bluebirds and cardinals as well as the sweeping fly patterns of the swallows. The older I get, the more I appreciate God's lavish creativity—his generosity in creating this splendid world I'm blessed to live in and blessed to share with my children.

God gave us birds to delight us. He gave us birds to teach us. The sparrow Scripture teaches us to trust him. Another verse a little farther on (Luke 12:24) teaches us we can depend on him: "Consider the ravens: They do not sow or reap, they have no storeroom or barn; yet God feeds them. And how much more valuable you are than birds!"

Birds are valuable, but we are more valuable. And what makes us more valuable is this: we are not created to follow programmed patterns of behavior but have been given free will. We were made to have relationship with our Creator, but we are free to choose it or let it go. We are free to give that relationship as much power in our lives as we choose. We are free to ask for divine help when we need it or to carry our burdens alone.

Likewise, we are free to build the kind of relationships we want within our families. And our children will eventually be free to reject or pattern their lives after whatever values we build into them during this long period of dependence.

We have true freedom to make the most of our mothering years—the freedom to envision what kind of family we want and then take the steps to make that vision a reality. What a blessing to those of us who grew up in broken, unhappy, or unwholesome homes! For while there may be a tendency to re-create the mistakes of our parents—just as the sparrows will build the same kind of nest their parents built—we're always free to do things differently, to do a better job.

If you hated growing up a latchkey kid, you may have promised yourself to stay home with your own children. If your mother wasn't a cookie-bakin' mama, you may have vowed to bake a couple dozen daily. If your mother was fanatical about housework, you may have decided to let your kids know they come before tidy closets and clean floors.

Isn't that a wonderful thing to know? I remember the moment I first realized it: my second daughter Jasmine had come home from school jumping for joy about an upcoming cake-decorating contest when I burst her bubble by announcing I wasn't the kind of mother who did that sort of thing.

It was when I saw the sadness settle in like a heavy cloak around her shoulders that I stepped away from myself for a moment and considered: how did it come to be that I had defined my motherhood this way?

Well, it was because my own mom hadn't been that kind of mother. As a single mother working two jobs—office clerk by day, cocktail waitress at night—to support three kids, my mom lost any spare time she might have had to problems with alcohol and men. Of course she didn't have time to decorate cakes.

But what was my excuse? I was a stay-at-home mom with two daughters in school. Yeah, I might not have been the most creative person in the world, but surely—since it meant so much to Jasmine—I could give it a try.

We made a Garfield cake with orange-colored coconut for fur. He won fifth place in second grade (not many people went home losers). I've kept my award and a picture of our Garfield cake. They mark an important moment in my motherhood—the moment I realized that I never again had to be limited by my past, that I could actually become any kind of mother I wanted to be.

If you're like me—and you probably are, because you picked up this book looking for ideas on how to be a better mommy just like I did way back in the beginning of my motherhood journey—you want to give your children roots and wings.

If you grew up in a good, strong, healthy family, your roots will be entwined with the generations that came before. If your intergenerational family's root system is weak or shallow or filled with decay, as mine was, you may be just beginning to put down fresh and healthy roots—beginning a process that will lead to a new family legacy.

When I speak of giving our children roots and wings, I'm talking about a foundation and a send-off. Though the send-off seems far away when you're still trying to keep from tripping over your little ones, the foundation-building that goes on till the day your child flies away on his own will have a lot to do with the quality of the send-off and the strength of his wings.

Wings are what take you out of the nest you were born in to start your own nest. And they take you out into the world to accomplish all the things you were meant to do. All the while we're bringing up our kids, we need to be preparing them to fly.

Does this sound a little too abstract? Too philosophical? Let me make it more concrete.

Like you, some mornings I wake up fighting off panic at all I have to do that day. I grab hold of God like a life preserver—"Lord, help me!"—and usually feel a certain peace. Then I look at all I have to do, and it all stretches before me in a way that seems doable.

But, believe me, it won't be long before something happens to upset the balance, and my plans for the day start wobbling like a house of cards. As memorialized in "By the Way," from a must-have children's CD by Joe Scruggs:

> It's Monday morning,
> I'm running late,
> There's not a minute to spare.
> Mom calls out, "Come on, let's go,"
> As she finishes drying her hair.
> Now I'm in my place with a smile on my face
> Just thinking about my day.
> Then I think of some things I'm supposed to bring
> And that's when I say,
> "Dear Mom, oh, by the way,
> I need an orange juice can,
> Four cotton balls, and
> Six rubber bands,
> And by the way, I'm an angel in the play.
> I'm going to sing
> And I need some wings."

A mommy's life is all about by-the-ways, isn't it? By the time the day is really underway, I'm starting to feel a little out of breath already, wondering if I'll make it to the finish line of bathtub and bedtime.

Though raising children may leave you as breathless as a one-hundred-yard dash, it's really more like a marathon. Analyzing parenthood from that perspective, I've come up with these "secrets" for finishing the race.

First, successful distance runners take the long view, see the big picture. They familiarize themselves with the course in advance.

23

How to Win the Marathon of Mothering

Think on the Big Picture.

Keep your eyes on the goal.

Acknowledge mistakes but keep moving forward.

Bring your best to each new moment.

They know exactly where they're headed and how to make it to the finish.

When they are discouraged, they remind themselves of crossing the finish line—focusing on that burst of triumph they will feel. In a long race, though the runners can't see it, their eyes are on the goal.

Sometimes they make mistakes. But when a runner falters—at the start, in the middle, even toward the end—she keeps going. She might even come back stronger. In other words, one mistake is not enough to ruin the rest of the race and perhaps may be the push she needs to finish well.

Finally, for the best runners, coming in first may be the goal, but more important is the satisfaction of knowing they ran their best race. Like Eric Liddell, the 1924 Olympic champion portrayed in the movie *Chariots of Fire*, who brought his best to each moment of the race because he ran to please the Lord, we can say, "When I run, I feel his pleasure."

When I do this mothering job well, I feel God's pleasure. I feel it even when I'm not at my best. I think God really likes it that we are taking care of the next generation of his creation.

And he knows we won't be perfect at it. Even in my worst moments, I can get a grip if I remember how good it's gonna feel when I stand before him, with the day-to-day tears and triumphs of motherhood far behind me, and hear him say, "Well done, good and faithful mommy."

The big picture of raising a child is this: because all your motherly ways and activities will eventually produce grown-up men and women, you need to consider what kind of men and women you want to produce. When you see the end goal, it's easier to take the steps and make the decisions that will help you get there.

Ironic, isn't it, how we need a license to do so many things in our society? A license to drive a car, build a house, cut hair, polish nails. But there are no requirements for being parents. And yet, for believers, the responsibility seems awesome, for God has entrusted us with the privilege of raising his children—because ultimately each one is his.

Becoming a believer revolutionized my motherhood, making me understand that it wasn't all about the day-to-day but about what gets passed down from one generation to the next. I love meeting believers who grew up in homes with a strong spiritual base, love hearing other women's stories of how their parents passed on the important things to them.

Since I already had five children when I started seeking God's direction for our family, I had to do a lot of catch-up. Pretty funny to remember myself learning Bible stories along with my kids.

But God had planted a few things early in my life that would be beneficial later on, especially as our family grew to twelve children (nine biological and three adopted). My training as a Montessori teacher taught me a lot about kids, about how they see the world and how we can meet their needs.

Now I've been a mother for thirty-five years, but with seven still at home I can't forget what it's like to be a busy mother of little children. I've had lots of years applying the principles I share with you in the pages to come. I've learned what works and what doesn't. And the absolute coolest thing—I've seen the results in my older kids as they've gone on to begin families of their own.

Families of their own—that was always the key. When I began to think about what kind of men and women I wanted to help my children become, I thought that first and foremost they should be equipped to be good parents. This meant they should love God and honor their own parents.

I wanted them to be kind and compassionate, thinking of others before themselves. I wanted them to be willing to help others in whatever capacity God calls them. Because our Creator made us in his image, I wanted to enable them to share in our creative heritage. And finally, I wanted them to take what their dad and I gave them and improve it, building an even better nest for their own families.

The Mommy Manual is my way of sharing all I've learned and put into practice. It's about life here and now with your children but also about helping them realize their potential to grow into men and women who will make you glad you had them.

This is a book that you can refer to again and again as your children mature and as new ones come along. The three main sections deal with three different dimensions of raising kids:

- Treasures—understanding your kids, releasing their joy—and yours
- Measures—building a good work ethic and gracious character in your kids
- Pleasures—passing on our cultural heritage and creating a rich family life

See, we are just so complicated! There's so much more that goes into making a mature human being than a bird. No wonder it takes twenty years rather than twenty days.

As for the baby birds outside our window, by the time they were fourteen days old, they'd grown feathers and were able to see. They were somewhat mobile and could teeter to the edge of the nest until they fell back in. Their squawking was more frenzied than ever.

On the sixteenth day, the nest was suddenly quiet, as though something was about to happen. The father bird stopped feeding the babies, instead perching a few feet away and chirping at them, while the mother continued to bring them food.

The next day the mother stopped feeding the babies. Both parents now flew short circles around the nest, chirping to the baby birds as if calling them to come out of the nest.

Finally, one of the babies edged its way to the brim of the nest, then jumped and half flew, half tumbled to the back of a patio chair, where it perched uneasily. Over the next few hours, one by one each of the birds left the nest. The parents continued to motivate them by perching a short distance away, calling to them.

Around our dinnertime, I checked and found all the new fledglings back in the nest, shrieking for food while the parents once again tried to keep up with demand.

The next morning, the flying lessons began again. As the fledglings grew stronger and more confident, the mother and father lured them farther away from the nest. But still not too far—maybe twenty feet.

Then back to the nest to wait for food from Mom and Dad.

And so it went for several days, until the fledglings had the strength to fly as hard and as long as their parents. And then they were gone, and the nest was empty. The parents had done their job and done it well. Without a single parenting book!

What surprised and impressed me was that the baby birds didn't just get up and fly away—it was actually a lengthy process requiring a great amount of stamina on the part of the parents. But it was a process defined by instinct.

We have to work much harder, I suppose. Ours is a much more lengthy and demanding process. And we can't rely on instincts but must gather information and make decisions, evaluating different "expert" opinions.

Just remember that when it comes to your child, you are the expert. Yes, it helps enormously to listen to the wisdom of others. Yes, it's good to have ideals to strive for in bringing up our children. But we should never let our ideals become sources of bitterness or discouragement when we don't quite measure up.

I share my own ideals not because I carry them out perfectly myself but because they are like lights shining on a path to keep me headed in the right direction. If I ever thought my words might add more burden to an already burdened mommy's life, I'd never write another word.

So promise me, as you read the chapters ahead: let your ideals lift you up, not bring you down.

To keep things in perspective, remember where your children actually came from. I mean, though a mother's body (yours or another's) bore them, they were really entrusted to you by God. That makes me believe—because God made us so unique and special—that each of us is the perfect parent for our particular children, that God specifically matched us.

And because God has different life plans for each child, he needs a wide variety of parents to raise them. That's why it's important not to compare yourself to other mothers or become a slave to one particular method. Instead, gather information and look to God for the final answers. He's given us an important mission, and we can count on him to guide us through.

Do you know God loves you? I mean, really know it deep down in your bones? Never lose sight of his love and compassion. He is not a critical parent waiting to pounce on us when we make mistakes. I feel certain he wants us to be confident in his love so that we can model it for our children through the way we parent them.

"So do not throw away your confidence: it will be richly rewarded" (Heb. 10:35).

The reward is this: raising children who can fly with confidence and grace.

And so we begin.

Think confidence and grace. Think roots and wings.

Part 1

Treasures

For where your heart is, there your treasure will be also.

Luke 12:34

1

The Keys to Joyful Motherhood

You wonder one minute why you had them and the next how you ever lived without them. They're exhilarating and exhausting—even at the same time. They bring out the best and the worst in you even as you're sifting through the worst and best in them.

You have children in your life. And once you have children in your life, you'll never be the same.

Like Dorothy in *The Wizard of Oz*—"Toto, I don't think we're in Kansas anymore"—it's as though you entered another dimension with strange sights (scribbles on the walls, beans pushed up noses), sounds (whining, wailing, the Wiggles), and smells (let's not even go there). It's a place you'll dwell in for what seems like forever even as more experienced mommies warn you how fast it flies by.

Only another mother can understand. My advice: surround yourself with other mommies. Go to MOPS or play groups.

Let the housework go and spend the morning in the park with other mothers and kids. Share your burdens and blessings with other moms.

There's nothing more calming and soothing than hearing another mother say, "I know how you feel."

And let me tell you right up front, I know how you feel too. Many days as a mommy, I'm just flying by the seat of my pants, dashing between dishes and diapers and deadlines. After all, I've been living the mommy life for thirty-five years. And though my Montessori training gave me a head start at understanding what makes kids tick, nothing could've prepared me for the surprises that daily living with kids could bring.

And nothing will require so much of you for so long.

If only we had ruby slippers! Then we'd dance down the Yellow Brick Road of motherhood! But even though it's not that simple, just having a road map can help you find your way.

Of course, a map of motherhood can't be real specific, because all mommies and all kids are different. But it can show you directions and landmarks and vista points and perilous places. It can take away the mystery and give you knowledge of the territory, making your motherhood journey that much easier.

The Mommy Manual is meant to be that map and more. This book will enable you to better understand your children, to find more joy in everyday life with them even as you are helping them realize all the potential with which they were created.

In the last decade we've seen magazine cover stories galore on how scientists and educators are waking up to the fact that the first six years are the most important in a child's formation. That means you are more than the sum of the many hats you wear as mother: cook, laundress, interior decorator, EMT, domestic engineer, social planner, personal shopper, waitress, chauffeur. More important than all these put together, you are your children's first and foremost teacher.

So even as you keep busy sopping up spills and slathering sunblock on shoulders, you're engaged in building the foundation of your children's character and teachability.

Sound intimidating? It's really not.

See, we tend to think of education as a teacher filling a child's mind with information. We think educators/teachers need to have certificates, be professionals.

But the word *education* comes from the Latin word *educare*, which doesn't mean so much pumping information into but instead drawing forth the potentials that are already there. Yes, eventually we learn facts and figures. But our education begins way before that, and it has more to do with setting up our character as well as our approach to life, learning, and others.

God has built certain potentials into each child—some shared by all children, and some that are part of a uniquely individual set of gifts. A mommy's job is to see these potentials and help them be released. It's not that complicated—just a few simple principles can keep you on track. And as you'll see, most of the process can be fun.

Keep in mind that this early learning isn't accomplished in a formal setting or with a rigid structure. It's just making a few changes in your environment and infusing your time with your kids with more encouragement for some specific qualities.

Even when or if you decide to turn over their formal education to professional teachers, remember you have been and will always be your child's first and foremost teacher. You are the person who knows your child best. Teachers will come and go, but you are consistently there to guide your child in the things that matter most.

No matter how good he or she is at their job, a teacher can never match the love you feel for your child. For mommies may be teachers, but our kids are more than our students—they are our treasures, like precious gemstones in a rough and primitive state, awaiting discovery by someone who understands their true nature and wants only to reveal their true beauty.

Believe in your children as treasures. See beneath the rough surface to the precious and priceless beauty God has given them. And when it's not the best of times but the worst, think of this story told of Michelangelo: when asked how he created his masterpiece sculpture, he replied he just chipped away at everything that wasn't David. I like to think that God is the master sculptor of our children, but we are like the chisel in his hands. In God's hands I can be patient as I do my part to help reveal the treasure he has planted inside each of my children.

Because of my Montessori training, I got hold of some keys that opened up some ways of understanding children I wouldn't have otherwise known. A few others I've found in my experience over the years. Others were added when I found faith in God. Today, I have thirty keys in all.

I like to picture them as jangling around on one of those enormous rings carried by British housekeepers in movies involving massive numbers of servants, tableware, and doors. I want them to be highly noticeable so I'll remember that when my kids are acting up or my temper's running short, all I have to do is pick up the keys to open doors and let more light shine on the situation—helping me to see things more clearly and to get unstuck so I can be the kind of mother I want to be, one who can unlock the treasure of my children.

Now I'm handing the first ten keys—five to unlock the mommy's potential and five to unlock the child's—to any mommy who wants to use them too. Try them and you'll open places in your motherhood and your relationship with your children you never knew existed.

Observation: Watch Them Well

My first homework assignment as a student teacher was to observe an animal at the zoo for two hours, taking thorough notes. I must admit I was resentful. What did this have to do with teaching kids?

Eventually I realized it had everything to do with it, because the assignment was actually an introduction to the art of observation. The simple fact was this: despite my initial balking, after two hours of gibbon observation, I knew I'd learned more than a stack of books could have taught me.

For anyone who wants to understand children, observation is a must. To give them the best, we need to see our kids clearly. My teacher training went on to include hundreds of hours and pages of assigned observation of children—individually and in groups—in classrooms throughout metropolitan Washington, D.C.

Now I'm a mother. And years of motherhood have only confirmed how important observation is for understanding what makes our own children tick.

Observation is really the starting point for mommies who want to tap in to their children's God-given potentials. Think about it: how many times are we advised in Scripture to consider? Consider the lilies, the ravens, or the all-encompassing, "Stop and consider God's wonders" (Job 37:14).

God's greatest wonders are right under our noses, if we can just take the time to stop, look, and listen to them as they go about their small pursuits. If God uses the lilies and the ravens to teach us the things he wants us to know, I know he wants to use our children as well.

The Benefits of Observation

You will know and love your child more.

You will see not only how your child fits into the general patterns of development but also his unique qualities.

You will know the minute your child is ready to learn something new or when he needs a new angle on something old.

You will gain insight into patterns of behavior that might otherwise threaten to drive you crazy.

You will clearly see your child's strengths and weaknesses. You will know exactly how to pray for him.

Mommies don't have a lot of extra time, so we just need to seize opportunities when we can. While you're busy with dishes and your child is absorbed in emptying the cabinets, take a few moments to focus on the details that make her the unique person she is. Ask God to help you see your child the way he sees her.

Two-minute snatches grabbed here and there throughout the day, if done on a regular basis, can be enough to establish a habit of observation. Soon you'll have the skill of a "professional" teacher in observing your particular child.

Being a committed observer also helps you avoid the trap of labeling a child then failing to notice when the label no longer fits. You'll perceive the slightest shifts and changes in his behavior, attitude, and abilities. This gives your child more room to grow and change. It also keeps your prayers fresh and up to the minute, so you can rejoice for each small improvement, each little victory.

My daughter Sophia, at three, had a whine that set my teeth on edge. Together we built a useless pattern. At the first few notes of her whining, I'd say, "I don't listen to whining." Then, try as she might, she'd be too frustrated to produce anything better. I was beginning to fear she'd someday leave for college without ever conquering the Dreaded Whine!

But I found a special time to talk to her about whining and why she needed to stop. We practiced saying things with a whine and without. Then we prayed together that God would help her with this problem. After all, children's problems are as big to them as our problems are to us. They need all the help they can get.

The next time Sophia started to whine, I felt my habitual response on the tip of my tongue. But then I caught myself because I could detect an ever-so-slight difference in her tone. She really was trying not to whine! Wanting to encourage her progress, I gave her a hug.

"Thank you for not whining!" I said.

Now her voice dropped a few more notches as she told me what was on her mind.

Think about what happens when you decide to break a bad habit. Sometimes the break is dramatic, but more often, change comes in increments—a little at a time. This happens with children too.

Watch your child carefully, especially when she doesn't know you're watching. How does she like to sit? What does she like to do? What evokes her power of concentration? Does she need to slow down or to speed up? Would it help if she held her crayon differently or placed her coloring book at a different angle? What frustrates her, distracts her, makes her worry? What produces a look of accomplishment, a sigh of satisfaction? What is her biggest problem? What brings out her best? Is she ready for a challenge? What can you do to take her to the next level?

Observation also makes our hearts more tender toward our children. Before your married life was filled with children and other distractions, did you ever grow tired of looking into your spouse's eyes? Think of the hours you spent gazing at your first child and bonding with him.

So forget the messes and the madness whenever you can. Capture as many moments as possible to observe each of your children, asking God's help in seeing what needs to be seen.

Then you'll know and understand your child as never before.

Understanding: See the World Their Way

Have you ever seen a ten-foot-tall chair? I've seen two—one at the Exploratorium in San Francisco and one on the way from my house to Winchester, Virginia, at a roadside produce stand.

Why would someone make a ten-foot-tall chair? I have no idea.

But those chairs have been an inspiration to me, reminding me how the world must look to toddlers. I imagine the challenge of climbing up to sit in the seat, then the insecurity of sitting there with my legs dangling in midair.

How different our little ones' perspective of the world is! How strange to be surrounded by grown-ups' legs! And what a strain—all that looking up and pulling on skirts and pant legs. You've got to admire the hard work that must go into coping with the out-of-proportion world in which they live. No wonder they're so worn out at the end of the day!

My point is this: in our busy lives, with so much important, grown-up stuff grabbing our attention, how often do we look around to see the world our children see?

Probably not often enough.

The result: though we occupy the same planet, live in the same town, share the same home, and move through the same rooms, our worlds are worlds apart. The distance in the perspectives from which we see things creates constant friction in our relationships with children.

It's up to us to bridge the gap. To understand kids, we first need to step into their very small shoes, cope with the king-sized obstacles they encounter, and process it all with their unsophisticated thinking.

It doesn't come naturally to see things from a child's perspective. How often do we lose patience with children, forgetting that though

Children Hear Differently Too!

Ever hear things differently than your child? I remember one Christmas as the Curtis kids watched Daddy putting the lights on the tree while they waited not-so-patiently, jiggling their boxes of ornaments.

At four, Sophia was having the hardest time.

"Are we almost ready, Daddy? Can't we just hang one, Daddy?"

"Just a few more minutes, Sophia," Tripp replied patiently. But after a few more "Daddy, plee-eeases" his patience was shot.

"Sophia, hold your horses!" he said.

Bewildered, Sophia looked at her box of ornaments, then all around the room.

"But, Daddy, I don't have any horses!" she finally said.

You can't take anything for granted with children. They are very practical; they take things literally. To avoid misunderstandings, you have to hear it their way. No ironic twist, no cliché, no figure of speech is safe!

we occupy the same territory, our experiences are vastly different? How frustrating it must be for them when we don't understand that the tasks we find so simple and automatic are complex and time-consuming for them.

As mommies, we're in a perfect place to make their world more secure, simply by understanding the daily struggles they face just climbing up to their chairs at the table or putting on their clothes with all the sleeves, legs, and buttons in the right places.

I think of it as Parenting by the Golden Rule: do unto your children as you would have done unto you. Recognizing their limitations, you can treat your children with dignity and avoid demeaning or belittling them. You can treat them with the same courtesy and consideration you show other adults.

All it takes is remembering to put yourself in their place, to try to understand the difficulties they face, to see the world through their eyes.

"But you're so patient. That's why God gave you such a large family." "I could never have so many children—I just don't have the patience." I hear these remarks all the time.

I am grateful for patience. Lord knows I need it! But really, I don't deserve the credit at all.

I actually started out the same as every other mommy. But God gave me a lot of kids. Through the years I've become patient as a result of living with them.

Let's face it: we all could use more understanding, more patience in every area of our lives—on the freeway, in crowded grocery aisles, in long lines at the post office. Having a big family seems to be one way to develop the kind of patience that will sail you through the day-to-day difficulties that still frustrate the less encumbered.

However, no one needs to have twelve kids to develop patience.

The first step is simply to see patience as a worthwhile and attainable goal. If you've been looking at the world as made up of two kinds of people, the patient and the not-so, just know that any mommy can become more patient with willingness and prayer.

Finding the kind of quiet time other women talk about has not been easy for me. But through the years of dishes and diapers and laundry, I've managed to spend a lot of time reflecting on the qualities of Jesus while going about my daily tasks. One reason I don't mind housework is because it frees my mind for greener pastures and stiller waters, like the ones David spoke of in Psalm 23.

I've thought about patience and how Jesus modeled it for us so well. The people who tried his patience were not those who made mistakes but those who laid heavy burdens on others, expecting more from them than their heavenly Father would.

When I think of how patient God has been with me through some of my stubborn times, I want to do my best to give my own children no less.

Observing, loving, and learning more each day about what makes your children tick—the reward for all of these is more patience and more peace in your home.

Example: Look Out for Little Mirrors

"Joshua, that's the third bowl of cereal you've spilled this week!" My first son's shoulders slumped at my shrill words. I could see he felt like a failure.

That wasn't how I wanted him to feel. I just couldn't understand why he seemed unable to carry his cereal bowl from the kitchen counter to the table without making a mess.

"Next time, use two hands!" Now I felt like a failure as well. Even as I jerked a towel from the drawer and impatiently started cleaning up, I knew I was the one in the wrong.

Have you ever been upset over spilt milk? Or apple juice, Cheerios, paint, or bubbles? Ever felt your temper rise—whether you lost or kept it—when a dish was broken or mud was tracked in? Children's carelessness is a constant source of frustration to us.

But one thing children are long on is forgiveness. Josh was off on some adventure, with the spilt cereal and my unkindness long behind him, while I was still mulling over the situation in my own prayer closet—my laundry room.

My teacher training had taught me never to undermine my students' confidence if I wanted them to succeed. Why should it be any different with my own children? Didn't I want the best for them? Why didn't it come naturally to apply time-tested teaching principles in my own home?

That morning I was convinced that the tools God had given me in my training as a teacher were not meant to be set aside when I became a mother. God wanted me to use them now more than ever—in fact, maybe that's what they had been intended for all along!

As a teacher, I had learned the importance of modeling careful movement—slowing down and exaggerating the care needed for a particular task—to maximize the opportunity for success.

Now at home Joshua was really my Little Mirror. If he was clumsy in the kitchen, it was because I should have realized that I could not habitually carry a cereal bowl with one hand while expecting him to carry it with two.

Children look up to us—we're their heroes!—and are influenced by our slightest movements and gestures. How often have you been startled by an all-too-familiar mannerism unconsciously mimicked by someone half your height? It might have brought you amusement or shame, or a mixture of feelings.

My son-in-law Kip told me this story. After eighteen-month-old Timmy's bath, Kip bundled him in a towel and headed for the bedroom. As he passed the living room, he tossed a hairbrush over to the couch so he could sit and comb Timmy's curly red hair once Tim was diapered and jammied.

"Before the brush was halfway across the room, I realized my mistake, but it was too late!" Kip said.

Sure enough, the minute Timmy was off the changing table, the little guy darted into the living room, grabbed the brush, and gleefully threw it across the room like a Frisbee, just as his daddy had done.

Just another Little Mirror.

Want a challenge? Begin observing yourself. How do you move about your kitchen? Do you dart from one distraction to another? Is setting the table a balancing act with a stack of plates in one hand, a tower of cups in the other? Is your mind on what you're doing or on what you're going to do?

When we are willing to see ourselves through our children's eyes, we begin to see how much we are at the root of their problems maneuvering through life. What happens when they're in a hurry, unconscious of what they're doing, or when they're trying to do more than one thing at a time? More often than not, they fail; and we of little patience just can't seem to understand why they can't do such simple things right.

Children are born imitators. God made them that way for a reason. He wants them to model themselves after their parents—the simplest and surest way to build a foundation. What an awesome responsibility for us! We can't ask our children to stop imitating; instead, we can become better role models.

Translated into everyday activity, this means you should use as much concentration to do something as your children need to do it. When they're around, you might spend more time than you actually need to do the simple things. You can walk more slowly when you carry something. You can carry smaller amounts and use two hands. You can open and shut doors and drawers more carefully. You can tie their shoes as though it were the most absorbing activity in the world. You can try to do only one thing at a time and be completely focused on the task at hand.

This discipline helps us appreciate the significance of the insignificant details that make up the fabric of our lives. Isn't it exciting to know that with just a little more attention to detail you can model tasks in ways that can help your children maximize their successes and minimize their messes?

Don't underestimate the significance of the little things. Think of it as behind-the-scenes education, every bit as important as the math and language lessons your children will receive in years to come.

And believe me, you will make up for the extra time it takes to slow down a little with lots less spilt milk to cry over.

Flexibility: Be Ready to Change

Once upon a time before I was a megamom, I taught in an inner-city Washington, D. C., school filled with kids from homes below poverty level. Entering school at age two-and-a-half with few language or social skills, they were like absorbent sponges, eagerly soaking up whatever was placed before them. They were wonderful, delightful, and challenging children!

Always looking for ways to enrich the environment, we subscribed to a visiting pet program. Each week, a van delivered three animal cages, one for each classroom.

Inside were the special visitors—birds one week, mammals the second, and so on through the five animal classifications. This was exciting for the children, many of whom had never had any up-close-and-personal exposure to animals. They thoroughly enjoyed the parakeet the first week and the hamster the second. They were eager for the third week's visitor.

But the teachers and assistants were worried, because the third week was reptile week, and each classroom would be getting a snake. Yuuuck!

The fateful day came. To allow them to acclimate to the new surroundings as peacefully as possible, the pets-of-the-week were delivered on Friday to spend a quiet weekend before the kids came in on Monday morning. So after school on Friday, three rather small garter snakes in three cages were picked up from the office by three grossed-out teachers.

Double yuck, I thought as I set mine on my desk. A city girl, I'd never been this close to a snake before and was not at all thrilled with the prospect of showing it to my students Monday morning.

However, there was a tension within me between my aversion and the challenge it presented. After all, I'd been assured the snake was harmless and that the children would be able to enjoy holding it. It didn't seem right to be so bound up by fear.

I braced myself and, lifting the screen top, gingerly touched then lifted the little snake from its resting place on a piece of gnarled wood. I was surprised at how smooth his skin was, not at all as I had expected. The snake seemed somewhat nervous, but as I remained very still and grew a little calmer myself, so did he. By the time I put him back, I knew I was ready for Monday morning.

Monday came and so did circle time. After a careful demonstration of how to handle the snake, I allowed the children to pass him around. Not only did they respond well to the new visitor, but they also thoroughly enjoyed the challenge of learning how to make him comfortable by being calm themselves. By the time he was returned to his cage, our snake had found a place in our classroom's heart.

But, oh, were we in for a surprise on the playground! While my students were bubbling with excitement about our pet of the week, the children from the other classes were aghast to hear that we had actually touched it. Their teachers, in not overcoming their own feelings of fear and disgust, had passed on their negative feelings.

What a vivid picture of our Little Mirrors! While I've talked about the importance of slowing down and moving more carefully to optimize our children's chances of success, there is a whole other area besides our outward actions that calls for our best role-modeling. That is in our attitude.

The snake experience taught me how important it is to take a good, hard look at all my own limitations so as not to pass them on.

And I had to do more than just grit my teeth and force myself to hold the snake. I had to make peace with it or the children wouldn't be able to.

With God, it's all or nothing—to be authentic, our actions have to line up with our hearts, so we can present a straightforward picture to our Little Mirrors, one that will reflect back their brightest and best.

How overwhelming and humbling that God has entrusted us with the awesome privilege of shaping our children to be the best they can be. But that carries with it the responsibility to be the best we can be.

Here's another challenge: as you spend a day observing your actions, why not spend a few days observing your heart?

Prepare with prayer, asking God to illuminate anything that stands between the children he's entrusted to you and all that he has planned for them. Do you have fears that are ready to be let go? Do you have bad habits of the heart, unwholesome attitudes that have been there so long you have forgotten to think about changing them? For those of us who come from non-Christian or unloving backgrounds, it's imperative that we be willing to leave no stone unturned in our self-observation. For those from secure Christian backgrounds, the struggle may have more to do with complacency or pride.

In his gentleness, God may reveal only a little at a time. We need only ask each day, "Create in me a clean heart," and he will continue to shape us as we shape the children he has entrusted to our care. In this way we will become more gentle, patient, and filled with joy each day.

Isn't it wonderful how God designed this to work? In learning to become better parents so as to help our children be the best they can be, we actually learn to be the best we can be as well.

Confidence: Be of Good Cheer!

Some people travel around the world, perfect their golf stroke or their makeup, or float through rooms right out of the pages of *Architectural Digest*. Others of us raise children—a brave and chaotic enterprise—dashing from doctors to Little League, clearing dinner dishes to make way for homework.

You may be reading this book with your first baby in your arms, just looking ahead to find out where you're going.

You may already have a toddler or two—and maybe a baby as well. You may have a string of kids from fifteen months to fifteen years.

Your most useful accomplishment each day may be to get the little ones to nap simultaneously so you can get a little rest yourself. Or maybe a shower?

You may be reading this book in snatches, between diapers and feedings and cleaning up the house, a page—or even a paragraph—at a time. I know. I've been there myself. I still am. I write in snatches, a page, a paragraph at a time.

Right now, maybe only for a little while, you have little children in your life. You may be frustrated because they often seem unfocused, aimless, or distracted. Perhaps they're not able to choose or concentrate on an activity and seem overly dependent on you for direction. Wherever they go, they leave a trail of clutter. Following behind, you're often so busy cleaning up that you despair of finding time to be the kind of mother you think you should be.

At the end of the day, do you ever wonder what it's all about? By then, you may be too exhausted to dream.

It's easy for mommies to get discouraged. There's so much work and so little recognition. No one gives you a report card or a performance review, not to mention a pay raise. No trophies, no awards, no medals.

That's why you need to notice and hang on to the little things—the fact that your five-year-old has finally stopped whining, that your preadolescent son cleans the kitchen after dinner without being asked, that your eight-year-old actually does his homework without finagling, that your two-year-old has learned to hug the baby without smashing his nose.

With eight of my twelve kids still at home, I know I have better odds than most of finding a little progress in someone's life each day: something that gives me hope, something that helps me remember why I had them in the first place, something that makes it easier to wake up the next day with a smile. But I started out like all young mothers, with lots of work and little reward, learning how to live with toddlers.

Remember that parenting is one skill that can be learned only on the job. One of the biggest problems of mothers is that sometimes when we learn something new, it becomes a source of discouragement as we start to measure ourselves against an impossible standard.

Be on guard against this as you go through parenthood. If you resist being too hard on yourself, you will never lose the joy of learning new things.

Begin by saying, "I will never be the perfect parent." Confidence is one of the greatest assets a parent can have. But note: confidence doesn't mean that you will do the job perfectly but instead that you have faith and are willing to do it to the best of your ability.

Yo Ho, Yo Ho, a Mommy's Life for Me

On a typical day as Mommy, I might be tired because someone was up all night with an earache. I might be looking at four loads of laundry and the dryer just broke and Sears can't come out until Thursday. My hyperactive daughter may be whining because she's hungry, even though she just finished breakfast thirty-seven-and-a-half minutes ago. The phone may be ringing, and I wanted the answering machine to get it, but four-year-old Justin is bringing it to me proudly after already answering it. There may be dirty socks on the kitchen counter, reminding me that I am powerless over whatever genetic component it is that makes boys shed socks all day all over the house, increasing my laundry time by 50 percent as I unroll each little ball before inserting in the machine.

Ay yi yi! If someone had handed me a job description like that, would I have chosen it?

When times are tough, I remember two things:

Dr. Dobson saying that love isn't a feeling but a decision.

And Mary Engelbreit's picture of a woman dancing with her vacuum and a feather duster. It reads: *To be happy, don't do whatever you like. Like whatever you do!*

As I said before, it's good to have ideals—but make sure they lift you up, not bring you down.

Remember when I compared motherhood to running a marathon? Well, even the best runners can't win the race if they're doubtful or discouraged. I believe God wants us to be confident, because then we're at our best. Confidence doesn't mean we think we can do the job perfectly; it just means we have faith and are committed to giving our best. Our confidence isn't found in ourselves or our parenting techniques, but simply in God. He is with us every step of the way.

2

The Keys to Joyful Childhood

Don't forget to have a lot of fun. Blow bubbles. Take walks together and collect leaves. Lie on the grass and look at the clouds with your kids. When it rains, run outside and get wet with them.

Though God is doing a lot of serious work in your children during the early years, he also wants them to jump and giggle and be surprised. If you think of something spontaneous and unexpected, don't put it off.

Do it.

We did it during a record-breaking heat wave one August in California. Because the Bay Area's coastal climate is mild, we were ill-prepared to deal with prolonged bouts of heat—no air conditioning, with fans few and far between. Four days of heavy heat and listless children were about all I could handle. On the fifth day I woke with a plan.

We headed off to the local rental store, where we rounded up a snow cone machine, cups, flavorings, and mountains of ice.

We came home and tried out the machine ourselves. It worked! After a round of snow cones, we all felt about twenty degrees cooler. And so we took that machine all over town: to job sites where my husband and his employees were valiantly trimming trees, to Pop Warner football practice, to special ed classes. Back home again we invited all the neighborhood kids to cool off with us. For three days, we made snow cones from sunrise to sunset. I don't think my kids will ever forget it.

Before the great snow cone adventure, I didn't know I had something like that in me. No doubt about it, parenthood has helped me to become a more spontaneous person. Our children can bring out the best in us, if we let them.

Now how can we bring out the best in them?

What are the potentials God has built into them? How can we help them be released and channel them in the right direction? How can we make the most of the early years so our children will become all they are meant to be?

Sensitive Periods: "Help Me Learn"

Children are created with such a drive to learn, they couldn't stop even if they tried. A toddler is abuzz with curiosity, poking and prodding, investigating anything and everything he meets on his wobbly way. If you've been watching, you've probably been amazed and delighted to see the intensity with which he examines his own small world.

The toddler's curiosity acts as a catalyst for new ideas, propelling him to try new things.

Think of what it means in the life of a child the first time he drags a chair across the room to find out what's on those oh-so-high shelves. A toddler's life is crammed with learning breakthroughs, and this is just one. He has recognized that he has control of the environment (at least as long as no one takes it away!) and can manipulate it to attain what he wants.

All over the world toddlers follow the same pattern of development, experiencing learning breakthroughs independent of the adults around them. As long as the environment is not unusually deprived, the child will attain certain developmental milestones following a more or less common timetable.

In our homes, it can look so normal and everyday. But when you think about it, how extraordinary!

Observing

It all begins with observation.

From those infancy moments when she follows your every move worshipfully with her eyes, to the time she's up and running—lugging a stool around the kitchen so she can watch you at work, learning all along the way—your child is an observer. Once a toddler decides she needs an up-close look at something, she is on her way.

No one needs to push a child to observe or to investigate; she does it because God built into her a drive to learn about the world. From infancy, before she can even reach for things, a baby is completely absorbed in the task of assimilating her environment visually, of using her eyes to make it her own.

Doing

Observation is just the first step, though, for God has also built into the child an overwhelming drive to do. What the child sees is just a motivator for acquiring motor skills. He reaches for the rattle first with his eyes, then with his hands. He notices some shiny keys a few feet away and scoots himself forward to capture them. He watches you peel carrots, and then he wants to do it himself.

When then two-year-old Benjamin discovered the dishwasher, he was fascinated by the connection between the switch and the sound of whooshing water. It didn't take him long to figure out how to start and stop the sound himself.

From then on, no dishwashing cycle was safe. The instant Ben heard the swoosh of the water, he'd toddle, full of purpose, from whatever corner of the room to pull that switch from right to left. Then, with a look of satisfaction, he'd toddle away, only to return the instant someone turned the machine on again.

He was a Man with a Mission! We so enjoyed his sense of accomplishment and good-natured acceptance of the machine that wouldn't stay still, that it often took hours to get the dishes done.

Doing is the second phase in the learning process. The child sees, then he does. And as each motor skill is acquired, it is immediately put to use mastering the environment.

It is in this second phase that things get tough for adults. Because as surely as toddlers are driven to *do*, we seem driven to stop them.

And so the toddler years come to be known, ungraciously and unfairly, as the "terrible twos." We fret and complain at our children's lack of compliance, at the messes they make, the disorder they cause. We find ourselves saying, "No, no, no, no, no," like a broken CD. We spend a large part of these years at odds with our kids.

I'm here to tell you things don't have to be this way. It is possible to thoroughly enjoy your children's toddler years!

First, you have to accept the doing—the toddler's drive to translate eyes-on to hands-on. Not that you should allow your children to run wild or get themselves in trouble, but you should try to lovingly understand what motivates their actions.

Doing is the toddler's mission. This is how God made her. It is in fulfilling her specific mission that a toddler finds her greatest satisfaction. She gains confidence as she learns to master her environment. She continues being drawn to the next developmental challenge. Before you know it, she wants to tie her shoes, answer the phone, and feed the cat.

She also wants to investigate how much water the bathtub will hold, see how much toothpaste is in the tube, and find out whether the baby will scream if she sits on him.

You can learn to read your child's motivations and respond in a way that channels her curiosity and energy in a positive direction. And along the way, you can discover ways to meet your child's needs so well that she will rarely find expression in negative ways.

The more you understand what's going on in your child's development, the more joyful and rewarding the preschool years will be. What's worked for me as a mommy has been the Montessori approach to releasing potentials God has built into each of my children, then using that foundation to support character building.

The immediate goal is to open the gateways to learning. The long-term goal is to produce men and women of character and purpose.

I came across the book *The Absorbent Mind* by Maria Montessori when my first daughter, Samantha, was a year old, so I had firsthand confirmation that her insights were correct. And after thirty-five years, through teaching in classrooms and raising my own children, I have more respect than ever for her work.

Maria Montessori, the first woman doctor in Italy, first chose to work with children in the slums of Italy. In the early 1900s such children were labeled "retarded." Montessori noted these impoverished children—with no toys and little stimulation—picking up crumbs from the floor to manipulate and play with. Their drive to explore and investigate despite their environmental limitations seemed close to miraculous.

And so she was inspired to develop a theory of child development and a method for making the most of it. The first ones to benefit from her work were the "retarded" slum children, who within a short time were outperforming their "normal" peers. Today, Dr. Montessori's ideas, which include such simple concepts as child-sized furniture, are incorporated throughout the world of early childhood education.

While today many people are touting the importance of the preschool years for optimum learning, I think it's important to give credit where credit is due for what was once—even as recently as thirty years ago—considered a radical idea.

Montessori's radical idea was basically this: that the preschool years are the most important years for laying the child's foundational attitudes. Nowadays that's not such a radical idea. But before rushing to put your kids in classrooms to take advantage of the learning power of the preschool years, take a deep breath and consider: all it takes is some understanding on the part of parents to get the same results.

While I will be sharing some of Montessori's basic ideas in this book, these ideas are also a springboard to the issues of character development. A mommy who understands what makes her child tick will find that character development will flow out of paying attention to what Maria Montessori called "sensitive periods."

Along with the drives to observe, to do, to master the environment, God has also built into each child certain potentials that will enable him to become a joyful learner, as well as a gracious and cooperative human being.

Each of these potentials has its sensitive period during the preschool years. This is a limited time when—if the conditions are right—the potential will become firmly rooted as part of the child's character. By right conditions, I mean appropriate environmental cues, plus loving parents or teachers who understand the child's drives and try to steer his course in the right direction.

This is not to say that a child whose sensitive period for order is missed will forever remain disorganized. But theory has it—and my experience agrees—that once the sensitive period has passed, only by a major act of the will can an older child or adult develop a character quality that could have come easily and gracefully in the toddler years. Worse yet, when the sensitive period is discouraged, or even trampled upon, we often see unhealthy, unproductive, and antisocial patterns in later years.

Sensitive periods could be referred to in today's language as windows of opportunity. That's a good word picture. When the windows are open, you can be part of the action inside; when they're closed, you're on the outside looking in. The windows are fully open for only a few years. In the preschool years you have access to the foundation of your child's character in a way that no one will ever have again.

As you begin to understand how these sensitive periods work in your child's life, you will probably find yourself becoming more patient around, more responsive to, and more satisfied with your child.

And as your understanding grows, you'll probably find your child becoming more patient, responsive, and satisfied as well.

Moms and kids can create vicious cycles—her obstinate behavior, my anger, more obstinate behavior. But by the same token, we can create the opposite, though I don't know that we have a name for it.

Harmonious cycles, maybe? It's what I aim for when one of my kids gets stuck in a stubbornly angry position. Instead of escalating, I choose to kneel down beside him and give him a big hug and sing "Hush Little Baby"—our family's favorite lullaby—into his ear. It's hard to stay mad when someone offers tenderness.

In the big picture, the harmonious cycle would look like this: as you find more joy and satisfaction in parenting, your child finds more joy and satisfaction too, thus bringing you still more joy and satisfaction.

If that's almost enough to keep you reading in between the runny noses and the loads of laundry, I hope it helps to know we're in this together! After all, I'm writing to you in between the same chores!

Independence: "I Can Do It"

"No, lemme dooit mysef!"

Sound familiar? It's the rallying cry of toddlers everywhere. At this very moment, throughout the world—in thousands of languages—children are telling their parents they want to do it themselves.

In Taiwan, Li Na is struggling with the buttons on her blouse, resisting her mother's efforts to take over and do it faster.

In Luxembourg, Jorgen's eyes fill with tears as his mother takes the pitcher from his hand—he wants to pour his own milk, sweet and fresh from the cow.

By the river in a remote African village, Kamaria pushes away two hands offering too much help and continues her efforts to balance the basket of fish on her head—just the way her mother does.

In Tokyo, Akira strains on tiptoe to unhook the latch of the gate, then sobs in frustration when his father reaches first and does it for him.

In Nebraska, Joseph collapses on the floor and wails when his big brother answers the door before he can get there himself.

"No, I dooit!" The words are simple, direct, and from the heart. They are also among the most frustrating mommies ever hear. Even worse are the wails and whines, clenched fists, squinched faces, flailing limbs, and melodramatic collapses our toddlers use to tell us how much they resent our doing things for them.

When these push our buttons, we may be at a loss for what to do. Often we find ourselves digging in our heels and making things worse.

In child development there is a universal language of independence. We as adults are on the other side of the struggle, but it would boost our mommy potential enormously if we could remember how we ourselves started. Because, as a matter of fact, everyone's march to maturity begins under the same banner.

In the beginning, each of us wanted to do it all ourselves.

See It Their Way

You want to put on your own socks. Your hands are small, but you're determined. You're giving it all you've got. The sock gets snagged on one toe and then another. Finally the sock has cleared the toes, and you're on your way to victory, and then . . .

Along comes a bigger pair of hands grabbing your sock and trying to "help" you.

"Hurry up! We're late!"

You don't know exactly what *late* means other than your mother is about to lose her temper. But there are these socks—

60

you can't think about anything else. Your existence has become focused on one need. You are compelled, pushed, driven to put these socks on your very own feet.

But these big hands are pushing your little hands aside and pulling the socks away. These big hands that are usually filled with love and understanding now offer only opposition. What recourse is there but to fight?

What life struggle would give you, as an adult, the where-withal to engage in hand-to-hand combat against an opponent packing five hundred pounds on a twelve-foot frame? Can you even imagine such odds?

How extraordinary that we mommies actually witness such displays of courage in our own homes each day! And all over little things like shoes and socks, buttons and barrettes, pitchers and sugar bowls.

Why do they do it? What could possibly give them the determination, the tenacity, the foolhardiness to persist in the struggle?

Get the Big Picture

Some might blame it on the fall, confusing the drive for independence with our flawed nature. And it is confusing, for the child's drive for independence begins around the age of two, when the effects of the fall are running rampant in their little personalities. That is why, mixed in with this very valuable potential for good—because the drive for independence is good—there is a lot of negative behavior.

But there is a difference between trying to pour your own cereal and making your mother chase you through the grocery store. The first is an example of wanting to take care of your needs, and the second is an act of rebellion.

Many parenting problems stem from lumping both types of behavior together, then reacting to either the same way. It's just automatic.

Mommies can't afford to react automatically, at least not if we want to help our kids grow into all they are meant to be.

So when you're faced with a standoff and you feel your impatience rising, try a fresh approach. Take a deep breath. Then, before reacting, ask yourself if the child's behavior is rebellious and destructive or whether it is the natural result of his drive for independence. Does this stamping of the foot signal rebellion, or does it mean you need to take a second look at the situation to see if it's an "I dooit myself" issue?

The ability to discern between rebellion and the drive for independence is key, because mommies need to be doing two things at once: setting boundaries to curb negative behavior and keep the children safe, and encouraging their drive for independence in a positive direction.

The drive for independence usually begins with self-reliance skills. Your little guy wants to do things for himself, like taking off and putting on his own clothes—sometimes several times a day. He's always looking for a new challenge, like getting into and out of his own car seat or cracking the eggs open for breakfast.

These are good things, things you want to encourage, even if it means a few elusive eggshells in the scrambled eggs. Even if it means constantly refolding clothes and putting them away—or better yet, teaching him to at least shove them in the right drawer (sooner or later, hopefully, you'll give up worrying about how the contents of your kids' drawers look—it will be crowded out by other things, believe me).

In just a few pages, I'll be sharing with you ways to help your children accomplish the things you may feel uneasy about letting them try.

Think Ahead

But first I want to get you excited about your child's developing self-reliance, give you a glimpse of the future, and share with you the benefits of raising a child whose independence needs have been met at the proper time.

A child who is not given opportunities in this area at this special time will be a child who struggles later on with independence issues. He may remain dependent on others to direct him through life. At the other extreme, he may eventually become the rebellious teenager, driven to assert his delayed independence in antisocial ways.

By contrast, the toddler whose parents have paved the path to healthy independence will have what it takes to become a self-reliant child. She will enjoy the satisfaction of doing things for herself. She will not be the one helplessly whining about the location of her shoes each morning, nor the one who needs supervision to get her homework done each night.

Independence is an essential building block of character, one whose presence or absence becomes very apparent during the teen years. A child whose independence needs were met at the right time in the right spirit—with appropriate boundaries—will grow into a teen you can count on. That teen will have a true independent spirit, with no axes to grind and an ability to make decisions based on his own values rather than those of his peers.

Healthy independence, together with godly values, enables an individual to go against the flow—that is, to do what's right when everyone else is doing what's wrong.

Understanding the long-range benefits of independence can help a mommy take a different approach to what people ungraciously call "the terrible twos."

How To's

One night years ago I turned on the water for fifteen-month-old Madeleine's bath and, as part of the well-worn routine, turned to scoop her toys from the basket to the tub. But there she was behind me, bending, picking out one toy at a time, throwing each delightedly into the water.

Beaming broadly, full of toddler confidence, she radiated without words, *I'll take over from here, Mom.*

I got the message loud and clear.

Be constantly on the lookout for the next step your child can take in "doing it herself." By providing opportunities for your child to grow in independence, you will meet this need in positive and safe ways, thereby eliminating showdowns over things that don't matter.

What happens when your child's next step toward independence is not such an easy one to handle? For instance, what do you do when you come into the kitchen and find your three-year-old on the verge of pouring a glass of iced tea?

(a) scream
(b) break out in a cold sweat
(c) act nonchalant so he won't get scared and drop the pitcher, then artfully take it away
(d) say a quick prayer, smile encouragingly, and say something like, "Oh, are you going to pour your own? Let's practice pouring without spilling. Then you'll be able to do it yourself from now on."

Be alert to opportunities to stretch yourself in this area. Take a chance—when it's safe to do so—and help your child meet the challenges he sets for himself.

64

Most of all, relax and realize that spills are not really such a big deal.

Look at it this way: if you woke up tomorrow with a burning desire to water-ski, your friends would never squelch your desire by saying you weren't ready. Nor would they wait for signs of your becoming ready. Instead, they would offer instruction and pointers to maximize your chances of success. Before your interest wore thin, they would get you up on the skis. If you fell down, they wouldn't take away your water skis and complain about what a mess you'd made. Instead, they'd minimize your clumsiness, encouraging you to try again. That's how grown-ups treat each other when one wants to learn something new.

Think of this the next time your child thinks he's ready to do something, like pouring his own milk, and you think he isn't. Sometimes the only reason he's not ready is that he's never had an opportunity to try.

Keep in mind that, just like us, children want to succeed. Sometimes it's helpful to point out the pitfalls: "Try using your other hand to hold the pitcher from beneath . . . Aim for the middle of the glass . . . Don't forget to stop before the glass is full!" However, nothing is accomplished when you rush to take over—nothing except giving the child the reminder that you are the one who knows it all and can do it all.

Granted, there are many things young children cannot and should not do by themselves. And when the child's actions place him in danger, a parent must emphatically say no, acting swiftly to keep the child safe. Aside from those situations, though, there are many things children can safely do for themselves.

Unfortunately, when we are on automatic pilot, we often say no when we could say yes. So turn off your automatic pilot. Encourage your child's independence by looking for ways to make things possible for him.

Make Things Possible for Them

Take extra time. Making things possible may be as simple as slowing down a little. Being a parent of young children means you almost always were supposed to be somewhere five minutes ago. Because of the hurry in our own lives, we often find ourselves putting a shirt on someone who really could have done it herself. Make it a point to give your child the time she needs to do things for herself. When you're going out, plan an extra fifteen minutes to get ready. Give your child the time she needs to get herself ready in whatever ways she has mastered. Let her know you're counting on her. This kind of time invested in your child costs nothing but will pay off in big dividends later on.

Take extra care. Often there are little things we can turn over to our toddlers if we just teach them a little extra care. Would you be surprised if I told you your two-year-old can be taught to carry a cereal bowl to the table without spilling? All it takes is for him to see you do it first. Your thoughtful and careful modeling will make possible for him a small accomplishment that will bring him enormous satisfaction. Demonstrate by using two hands, watching the bowl as you walk, and walking slowly and carefully. Exaggerate! If you slow down and concentrate, your child will be mesmerized, I promise. Show how to set the bowl on the table before sitting down. Show concern about it being far enough from the edge not to fall off. Now let him try. Remember not to fill the bowl too full! Children are born imitators. The best way to avoid spills and messes is not by keeping everything out of their hands but by using exaggerated care in the little things they watch us do, then giving them opportunities to join in.

Use a fresh approach. Sometimes a task can be too challenging for a child to conquer even with extra time and extra care. Here we need to rethink a task to find a fresh approach. Take, for instance, putting on a coat. Even a two-year-old can do it this way: show your child how to lay the jacket in front of him, opened wide, with the neck closest to him. Now he can bend, put his arms in the sleeves, and flip the jacket overhead. The sleeves slide down the arms to the shoulders, and you just need to help with the zipper. But start those zipper lessons right away!

Give Encouragement

Always encourage your child's efforts, even when the results are less than perfect. A child learning to dress herself doesn't care so much if her shirt is inside-out. Wait until she's enjoyed putting on her own shirt a few times before a gentle "Oh, look at these buttons! Did you know that shirts have an inside and outside? How can we fix it?"

Of course, you want to spur the child to do her best, but use discretion. The first time a child accomplishes some task on her own is not the time to lower the boom. In encouraging her to improve, treat her with the same kindness and consideration you would a friend.

Beyond the toddler years, continue to look for ways to encourage your child's independence. As soon as he can tell time, buy him a clock and let him wake up to his own alarm and morning routine. Teach him to make his own breakfast or lunch.

Remember, the time you devote to fostering your child's independence is an important investment in the future. When you give him encouragement to "do it himself" during the sensitive period for independence, he will grow to be competent and confident.

An old maxim says, "Give a man a fish, and he will eat for a day; show him how to fish, and he will eat forever." As a mommy, I've found the greatest satisfaction watching my children's self-reliance grow as they depend on me not to do things for them but to teach them how to do things for themselves.

When you need a little extra patience to allow him to "do it himself," remember that because of your encouragement in the early years, your child will never be the one helplessly waiting for Mom to complete his seventh-grade science project!

Think of it this way: parenting is one job we should be working ourselves out of each day!

Order: "Where Does It (Where Do I) Belong?"

No one needs convincing that the toddler years are when the drive for independence is strongest. But would it surprise you to learn that the sensitive period for order is strongest at that time as well?

Mommies who spend their days bending, scooping up blocks, blankets, and baby dolls may be quick to disagree. I admit, because I'm still scooping up a few toys myself, it often takes a mighty stretch of the imagination to remember that the seeds of order exist in those busy bodies.

Seeds—that's really the best way to describe how the potential for order is built into children. If we think of independence as a wild vine growing nonstop in all directions—a vine that takes careful tending, pruning, and guidance to help it produce the best fruit—then, yes, order is dramatically different. Order is more like a tiny seed waiting for the right environment to allow it to flourish.

That environment is something we can provide.

Sowing Seeds of Order

First, take the long view. The nurseryman couldn't convince you to choose a seed packet and put special care into its contents without a picture of the fruit on the front. Likewise, it helps when you have a vision for where these potentials of your child are headed.

The potential for independence can produce some noteworthy fruit, if the child's needs are met in appropriate ways. In the previous chapter we saw that mature decision making and the ability to do what's right rather than what's easy or popular depend on this healthy foundation of independence.

The potential for order is of a different character. It produces something more like ground cover. At maturity, it doesn't attract much notice but provides a beautiful background for the rest of the garden. And when a slope is threatening to slide, it holds the soil together to keep the hill from crumbling.

How Order Provides Stability

When times are tough, when storms are knocking down the more conspicuous greenery, order may well be all that holds each day together until the storm has passed.

The most visible order in my life has to do with laundry. With so many kids and their many pursuits, I can accumulate a mountain of laundry if I stop washing for a day. Since it is easier to do the things I have to do if I stop loathing and start loving, I made a decision years ago to love my laundry. I also learned to spend that time with the Lord. I even wrote a book about it—*Lord, Please Meet Me in the Laundry Room.*

Now, because I've spent so many moments with God there, my laundry room has become my prayer closet, my hiding place, my anchor. Each day may be different, but one thing's for sure: there is laundry. And no matter how pressed I am for time, I can sing and pray while the clothes get clean.

When my son Jonathan was born twelve years ago, he had many medical problems. It was one of the most difficult periods of my life, with seven children at home and a tiny baby in a big university hospital. Trying to be there for everyone, I would wait for my husband to take over at the hospital each evening, then drive home, barely coping with the emotion and exhaustion.

After staggering through the front door, my steps became more purposeful as I made a beeline for my laundry room, too tired even to pray. Only when I had sorted the laundry, unrolled the balled-up socks, measured the soap, and heard the whoosh of the water could I relax and spend time with the children.

A superficial observer might have questioned my sanity. But no one would have questioned that I always walked out of my laundry room a little refreshed.

Now I see that as my world seemed to be falling apart and our family structure was so out of whack, I was holding on by a thin thread of laundry. It was the one event I could count on, the tangible thing that was always the same. It represented peace, stability, and order.

The Best Model of Order

Order is not an easy subject for some adults. Many of us struggle with order ourselves, or at least some aspects of it. We are disorganized, forgetful, or habitually late. We're set in our ways, and so we resign ourselves to our bad habits and may even be defensive of them.

So how does God see it?

I've often thought of God's act of creation and how he fashioned the world with order, accomplishing one specific task each day and finally resting when everything was complete.

I've thought of creation itself, how order is built into it, making life possible. The earth revolves at a precise distance around the sun, for example. Any nearer or farther and we would burn or freeze to death. The tilt of the earth's axis makes the seasons possible, year after year. The speed of rotation is consistent, giving regularity to our waking and sleeping. Gravity holds it all together. All was created with precision and a high regard for order.

If we're committed to giving our best to our children, we need to appreciate the purpose order serves in our lives. Just as the orderly precision of the universe keeps it running smoothly, so too does order on the human level make for ease of living.

Webster's *New World Dictionary* has twenty meanings for order. The second definition is "a state of peace and serenity." Is it only coincidence that the next two definitions are "the sequence or arrangements of things or events" and "a fixed or definite plan, system, arrangement"?

No, not a coincidence, according to my experience. I am certain that we find peace and serenity in environments that are planned and arranged with an eye to order.

Bringing Order to Your Home

MAKE A DECISION

As I said before, order—though a God-given potential in each child—is not of the same character as independence. The child's need for order is not so powerful. You don't find yourself butting heads with it, seeking to stifle it, coming to grips with it.

The potential for order lies in wait like a dormant seed within the child. You'll see signs of it only when it's planted in the right soil—soil that has been properly prepared to encourage its growth. Once the seed has sprouted, you will need to give it a lot of attention and care to keep it alive and well. It may not be the fastest-growing plant, but once established it will surprise you with how little maintenance it requires.

In more practical terms, if parents provide the proper environment and encourage the child's potential, if they are patient and persistent, they will see wonderful results: a child with a strong sense of order, a foundation for peace and serenity.

If order is not something that comes easily to you but you understand the benefits to your child, remember you can change! Our children's character and future are worth any amount of effort to be the best we can be.

The first step is to make a decision. The second step is to aim for order in your own life and the running of the household. The third is to fit the environment as much as possible to meet the needs of the child.

SEE IT THEIR WAY

I'm not suggesting that the world revolve around your child. But your home is already equipped to meet the needs of adults. It might be interesting to spend a little time seeing the environment through your child's eyes.

Earlier I mentioned the giant chair as a reminder of how our world must look to children. As recently as thirty years ago, it was virtually impossible to find child-sized tables and chairs except through school supply houses. Now you can pick up child-sized furniture at any discount department store.

Still, there's a lot in a toddler's life that's out of proportion and confusing, and the more we understand their needs, the better we can provide for them.

Putting myself in the place of a toddler, I imagine a world where I have to stand on tiptoe and swipe my hand blindly across the surface of a shelf to find out what's up there—only to get in trouble for spilling or breaking something. Where someone takes my jacket and hangs it up for me when it would be so nice to be able to reach the hook myself. Where all the excitement seems to be happening on the kitchen counter, too remote for me to see.

No wonder God built kids with a compulsion to climb! Otherwise they'd collapse from frustration or boredom.

Have you ever wondered what it feels like to sit at the kitchen table to color, feet dangling helplessly from a booster seat?

And what about these toy baskets? If a toddler could speak, he might say something like this: "This toy basket comes up to my waist. I can't find anything in these heaps of toys, and so I dump them all out; but that seems to make everyone pretty unhappy, especially when it turns out there wasn't anything in there I wanted to play with anyway. What are these baskets here for?"

Create a Child-Friendly Space

A child can't tell us these things. And by the time we grow up, we've forgotten how desperately small and inconsequential we felt in relation to the world we lived in. One reason young children love going to preschool is because there they finally enter a world where their needs are met.

With just a few adaptations, we can make our homes much more child-friendly. A child-friendly space is related to order, but it also meets independence needs and security needs. Think of how much freedom and security we have in an environment scaled to our needs. Then think how little our children have.

Keep in mind with the suggestions that follow that many aspects of the child's developmental needs are woven together in creating a child-friendly space. As each item is discussed, think how it would work to make the child more self-reliant, secure, and self-confident.

- **Incorporate child-sized furniture.** Start with the basics. This means a place to sit and work that fits and feels comfortable. A child-sized table and chair set is an investment you'll never regret. Your toddler is sure to be delighted by furniture tailored to her proportions. For endurance, wood is best—mine has lasted through eight children. If new furniture is beyond your budget, check garage sales and secondhand stores. There are also sturdy plastic sets available at discount toy stores. Once you know what your children need, God has a way of providing it at a cost you can afford. Once you bring the table and chairs home, do not put them in your child's bedroom, where they will only collect dust. Instead, put the table and chairs where the life of the family is centered, someplace where she can do things and still be very much a part of the hustle and bustle of daily life. Not only will she use them often, but you will have the satisfaction of seeing your child at work.

- **Create a special workplace.** Even if you're short of space, look for just a corner that can be a special work area for your child. You may have to come to grips with some preconceived ideas about home decorating, but the sooner you drop your aspirations to have a designer house the happier everyone in the home will be. Besides, we can all be perfectionists later to keep ourselves busy and take our minds off Empty Nest Syndrome. Finding a spot for your child to work comfortably, without being separated from the rest of the family, is top priority in the preschool years. Sooner than you can imagine, privacy will become a new priority for her. Then you'll wish she wasn't always disappearing into her bedroom.

- **Employ a kitchen stool.** Another way to enjoy more companionship with your child is by bringing him up to your level in the kitchen. A stool next to the counter will open a whole new world to him as he watches you sift, measure, mix, and pour. If you are concerned about safety when you're not around, stash the stool in a closet. Just don't get too hurried to bother getting it out. Try not to miss these precious moments when you and your child can see things almost eye-to-eye.

- **Decorate in child-friendly ways.** When I came across a loveseat covered in a Grandma Moses–type pattern (farmhouses, cows, chickens, and dogs), I snatched it up—not so much for me or my husband but because the pattern made me smile to think of how much my kids would love looking at it. Beside the loveseat, I set a display table with a heavy glass top and slide-out display drawer; instead of putting anything impressive in it, I arranged my children's assortment of fast-food freebies. Facing the loveseat is a stand of children's books; it's not surprising that this whimsical oasis has become a favorite spot for a good read. Even in the living room, our coffee table holds children's art books and magazines rather than adult reading material. I can always think of where to find something to browse through, but my children need things up close and personal to grab their interest. When I buy pictures, I choose ones interesting to my children too. Surprisingly, children love classical art, perhaps because they will often spend enough time looking at the picture to get the whole story; the toddler years are the perfect time to begin to stimulate in your child a lifelong appreciation of art. (Look for more on this in the Pleasures section of the book.) Don't forget to hang at least a few pictures (and a mirror or two) low enough for your child to enjoy too. And for even more affordable art, try greeting cards. They are so beautiful, and inexpensive frames so plentiful, that you can create many miniature artworks for next to nothing. Then think of yourself as three or four feet high, take a trip around your house, and find all the nooks and crannies where your children will be sure to notice them.

Even if you find this inspirational—in a fun kind of way—you may be wondering how this relates to order and to the child's development. Here is the connection: our surroundings say something about us. That's why some of us spend a little too much time decorating, and why your house looks different from your neighbor's. The environment also sends a message to children. Usually it tells them they are helpless and unimportant. If their personalities don't impact the environment, they could feel like they're just passing through, much the same as you or I might feel in a hotel.

A child-friendly environment sends a much different message. When the home is ordered in such a way as to take the needs of the child into account, it gives your child assurance that he is a vital, contributing member of the family. For instance, a stool in the kitchen tells your child not only that you trust him but also that you welcome his company. A picture hung at his level tells him you care.

Just as important, these things communicate something about the child's place in the world. They give him a sense of belonging, of "fitting in." In this way, a sense of order begins to be established in the child.

The best learning takes place in an environment that is comfortable and secure, built on a foundation of order. Making our homes child-friendly is like adding nutrients to the soil to better nurture the seeds of order in our children.

Instill a Love of Order

Now we need to dig deeper. Since our children are Little Mirrors, our own ability to keep order in the environment is essential. Here's where the soil may need more than nutrients—it may need a Rototiller! If order isn't your own strong point, it might help to think of how it would make your own life easier if it were.

One of my sons, now grown, is a terrific guy in many respects: bright, cheerful, fun to be with. But as he was growing up he struggled greatly because of his lack of order. He lost time and temper when he couldn't find his shoes, his homework, or his football helmet.

Like any other mommy, I wondered what went wrong. After all, this son had the same mother and father, the same home as his brothers and sisters.

The truth is, nothing "went wrong." Though the potentials exist in each child, each child is a unique blend of strengths and weaknesses. If we are providing all that we can to encourage the child's potentials, then we can be confident in the job we've done as parents. When children have problems later on, we can keep guiding them in the right direction, but we don't need to spend a lot of time feeling like we must have failed.

Even with the same seeds in the same soil, one plant can seem hardier than the one next to it. So you give the weaker one a little extra care. In my son's case, once the sensitive period was past, I had to encourage him to use his will, to make a decision to choose order in his life.

Have a Place for Everything

A child needs an environment that makes sense to him. When he is surrounded by order and when it is brought to his attention, he will naturally want to contribute to it. Seize that window of opportunity by giving him many ways to keep things in order. Begin by having a place for everything and everything in its place.

Put a peg rack at his height near the front door so he can hang up his own jacket when he comes in. A boot tray underneath will keep dirt off your carpets and help him remember where his shoes are.

Keep things organized in an attractive way. Life with children means life with all kinds of assorted odds and ends, so toy boxes and baskets will always be with us, but make them a last resort.

Opt for shelves whenever you can. White shelves are best because toys and learning materials look most attractive on a white surface, and children will be drawn to them. I buy white laminate shelves, thirty-six inches high and nine inches deep, that I assemble myself. The shelves are bright and easy to keep clean. Try to buy extra shelves (check for a store that has them available), so that one bookcase can hold a lot of organized stuff.

Put as many shelves as you can afford near your toddler's table, in his room, or wherever you want your child to spend time. Use baskets or plastic containers to sort and hold things like small blocks, beads and laces, pegs, whatever would otherwise be part of the jumbled mess in the toy box.

Now, teach your child to take out one thing at a time, to spend as much time as he wants with it, and then to put it back before taking out anything else.

Nurture a Lifelong Appreciation of Order

Order is also about pattern and sequence, and so we can reinforce the child's awareness of order by breaking down any activity into component steps, by talking things through from start to finish: "Should we make some carrot sticks? Okay, first we get the carrots out of the refrigerator. Now we need to get the peeler. Now we peel the carrot . . . The carrot's peeled, so now we can cut it into sticks. Now they're ready to eat!"

You see, that's how life really is, sequenced and orderly, one action following another. Order provides your child with a feeling of security. When she knows where to hang her jacket, where to put her shoes and toys, she feels less helpless and more competent.

Your understanding of your child's need for order and your loving provision will nurture this potential in her life and work. This will make it easier for her to accomplish all that she undertakes.

At the same time, as you begin making changes in your home to meet your child's needs, you may find yourself becoming more sensitive to order and to its benefits for each of us. You may develop a deeper appreciation for the order inherent in the world God gave us.

Then, even when you are overwhelmed by many demands, you may find a place of rest for your own spirit.

Self-Control: "What Are My Limits?"

A lot had been invested in this event before we even set foot in the razzle-dazzle building. Now Mommy and kids were finally here—at the San Francisco Symphony, eager for the annual Lollipop Concert to begin.

Our prep work had included learning not only about instruments and composers but also about sitting still and listening. I knew my kids were ready to get the most out of this unique experience.

We'd battled rush hour, seized a hard-to-come-by parking space (whispering a prayer of thanks), safely negotiated several crosswalks and numerous hustlers trying to share our money or their message, rummaged through Mom's purse to find the wayward tickets, made the obligatory bathroom rounds, and finally wound our way to our balcony seats.

As I sank into the rich plush velvet, I breathed a sigh of relief and gazed at the ceiling, a canopy tranquil as the clouds. I could have easily sat for days just soaking in the soothing colors and textures. The hectic few hours before began to melt away. If I had been thinking in words, they might have gone something like this: *What a gift God gives us to allow us the ability to rest, like throwing an exhausted swimmer a life preserver!*

Then I looked below at the rapidly assembling audience as clusters of twenty-some children, freshly dropped from school buses all over the Bay Area, began to turn the tidy rows into a vast and churning multicolored sea. A frothy, foamy surf of tapping legs and jerking arms, twitching hands and feet, bouncing shoulders and bobbing heads.

Here and there, like dolphins breaking the surface, children popped spontaneously out of their seats to grab a friend, to wave at someone down the row, or just for the sake of popping. Teachers tried sporadically to establish a bit of order but without much success.

Clinging to my own inner life preserver, I spotted a few randomly sprinkled islands of calm. These were classes from Catholic, Christian, and other private schools. I could tell by their uniforms. But more than that, I could tell because they were sitting calmly in their seats.

Pulling out my opera glasses, I scrutinized them up-close-and-personally. Like a scientific observer on a fact-finding mission, I had questions. What set these children apart? Why were they able to sit still? Were they unhappy? Afraid to be themselves? Had they been threatened with punishment?

Not as far as I could see. Instead, they seemed like normal, happy kids, perhaps even happier than the ones in constant motion. They weren't sitting in silence but were chatting with those nearest them, some girls comparing jewelry or smoothing their hair, much like adults waiting for a performance. Their teachers were not watching them like hawks or prison guards;

neither did they seem harried or overburdened or as if preparing for the next outbreak.

The longer I watched, the clearer it became that these kids, in general, seemed to be self-governed rather than dependent on the adults around them to keep them in line. It occurred to me that while the disruptive children seemed to have more freedom, the self-governed children actually had the truest freedom of all—freedom to govern themselves and their own actions.

What made the difference? How did some children become self-governing, while others were so dependent on outside control? Long after the first and last notes of the concert sounded, and in many quiet moments in the days ahead, I thought about the grown-up lesson I had unexpectedly encountered at the Lollipop Concert.

Raising Expectations

Popular wisdom tells us that people rise to the level of expectation of those around them. In factories and businesses, when companies expect more of employees, production and customer service are better. On fields, courts, and in arenas, coaches demand the best to produce star athletes.

In a similar way, our expectations of our children can help them become the best they can be. Expectation is vital to our vision of where our children are headed. It's not so much that we decide we want Johnny to be a rocket scientist or Megan to be an Olympic ice skater. We're talking about something more subtle and more important than career goals. We're talking about the kind of men and women we're preparing for the future.

Our training of their character and the day-to-day progress we make in helping them build it—that's where our expectations can and should be the highest.

Children were created with a potential for self-control. The sensitive period to begin realizing that potential is in the toddler years. But before we can do anything to see it released, we need to check our own attitudes and expectations and be ready to make any adjustments we might need to help our children become the kind of people God intends them to be.

First, we need to put aside any preconceived notions about children's capabilities and limitations. As a starting point, try mentally stepping back in time, or perhaps around the world, to think about what has been required of children in other times and other places. In many societies, children are given responsibility and treated as adults well before adolescence. Earlier in our own culture, children worked and participated fully in adult social life. Our current society is actually an exception in having created such a distinctly defined and prolonged period of childhood.

Here, we're looking for a more balanced view, one not bound to our own culture, which for years has been expecting less and less from children and is already paying the price. Yes, perhaps there were times when children were raised too rigidly, but our pendulum seems to have swung too far the other way. Now it seems anything goes: "After all, they're only children."

Is it only coincidence that as our standards for children have collapsed, we no longer see the Abraham Lincolns and George Washington Carvers we once produced in America? Maybe we need to stop looking at kids as "only children" and start seeing that they are our future, our inheritance, and the parents of the generation to come.

Maybe it's time to take the idea of self-control out of the attic and give it a good polishing. Is there something important we've been missing? Is there value in a row of children sitting calmly while waiting for a concert? What does it matter in the long run? And what does it have to do with producing men and women of integrity?

Let's go back and start at the beginning.

THE DEVELOPMENT OF MOTOR CONTROL

Turn your thoughts to the first months of watching your baby grow. Remember when his arms waved aimlessly, just moving for the joy of movement? You hung eye-catching things in front of him, and over time his arms' wide circles narrowed in scope, becoming more purposeful, until finally his hand made contact.

Even if this was a random event, the result was entertaining and definitely worth repeating. Gradually your baby perfected his aim. As he did so, he was exercising both his brain and his body—more particularly, the messages and coordination between the two. Soon he was 100 percent accurate in batting the toy. What child development specialists call "gross motor control" was being developed through concentrating on a target and practicing.

THE PROGRESSION FROM GROSS TO FINE MOTOR CONTROL

Over the next few years, you witnessed the refinement of your child's motor control from gross to fine. Where gross motor control is waving a rattle, fine motor control is picking up a Cheerio with a sticky finger and putting it in his mouth or capturing a tiny feather and twisting his hand to examine it from every angle. To properly develop both gross and fine motor control, a child must be developmentally ready and must have an environment that offers opportunities to practice.

My son Jonny, who has Down syndrome and is twelve years old as I write, has given me the opportunity to study more closely the intricacies of motor development. Other children make progress in leaps and bounds. We take their development for granted. But with children like Jonny, every part of the process takes on greater individual significance as we are required to put more thought, care, and practice into helping him achieve each small developmental step. From lifting his head to sitting to walking to climbing the stairs—each skill has taken many more hours of practice to master.

Observing Jonathan has also shown me that gross motor skill is virtually indispensable to fine motor. Because he was delayed in his ability to sit on his own, Jonathan was not able to use his arms to play as a sitting baby would; with no practice, his fine motor control would have been even more delayed. To compensate, we sat him up with his back straight while encouraging him to hold light rattles. Thus, when the time came for him to feed himself, he was strong enough to lift a spoon because of all his early practice.

The Relationship of Motor Control to Self-Control

There are parallels between the young child's development of motor control and his later potential for developing self-control.

FROM GROSS MOTOR CONTROL TO FINE

A child progresses from the big and obvious movements to the smaller and subtler—one builds a foundation for the other. A child developing self-control follows a similar pattern.

PRACTICE TO MAKE PERFECT

Just as in motor development, the child needs opportunities to exercise his limited powers of self-control to prepare him to gracefully handle the unexpected.

Let Them Know What You Expect

In day-to-day situations—at home or when going to the grocery store, church, or the library—Tripp and I have found one small thing to be of enormous benefit. We let our children know clearly beforehand what our expectations are for their behavior.

For example, on our way to church, we remind them that there will be only one trip to the bathroom—before the service starts; that we will be sitting together as a family; that we expect them to sit still, listen attentively, and participate fully; that they should refrain from rattling their bulletins or bothering those around us with unnecessary noise; that when the time comes to leave for Sunday school, they are to walk, not run; that they are to treat their Sunday school teachers with respect and other children with courtesy; that they are not to overdo it at the hospitality table; that they are not to disappear when it's time to go home.

When they know what is expected, all it takes is a glance at someone who is out of order—you know the glance I mean. Not a glance that instills fear, just one that reminds them where they are and what the expectation is.

This is part of the process of teaching children to become self-governing rather than needing to be kept in line moment to moment by adults.

REFLECT EXPECTATIONS

Did you know that when children with Down syndrome were raised in institutions, the average age at which they learned to walk was seven? Now, raised in loving homes with parents whose expectations are higher, they learn to walk at two or so. This is parallel to the development of self-control in children. In general, children rise to the level of expectation of their parents and teachers.

Expectations influence a child's long-range level of performance. Also, as in the concert example, expectations can affect specific behavior.

Fostering Self-Control

For independence and order, taking the long view helps—and the same is true for instilling self-control. There are two areas of caution, though. First, make sure that what you're aiming for is genuine self-control, not conduct based on fear of punishment. Although in the younger years a child's behavior is controlled through discipline and respect for authority, you're trying at the same time to develop your child's ability to govern himself. Even if a child's behavior is consistently good, if it's always the result of control by others, he'll be vulnerable to rebellion when he is older.

BE REALISTIC

Construct your expectations realistically. Children are individuals, and to make things even more complicated, they're changing all the time. You need to know your child well and to have an accurate picture of her capabilities. Observe, observe, observe! Set your expectations high but never too high for your child to reach. Otherwise you end up with a discouraged child. Remember you can always rely on God for help. Ask for and receive his guidance in setting expectations and helping your child meet them.

BEGIN EARLY

These potentials—independence, order, self-control, and those we've yet to discuss—do not exist in isolation. There is an interplay and balance among them. Thus, when you provide your child with an orderly environment and opportunities to develop independence, you are also providing the best setting for developing his self-control.

Pouring his own milk and carrying his cereal bowl to the table require independence, a sense of order, and a lot of self-control. The more often you turn this sort of activity over to him, the more practice he will get. But also, just as you hung rattles in front of your child to teach him to reach specifically, you can provide your child with motivation and specific practice in the art of self-control.

Start with gross motor control. Use a balance beam or a line of masking tape on the floor to introduce your child to the concept of bringing his body under control. Show how staying on the beam or the line requires careful, slow, thoughtful movement.

Once your child has practiced and gained confidence with this, try the next exercise to challenge and refine his growing sense of self-control: walking with a bell.

A glass bell is ideal, because the clapper is easy to see, or look for a bell where the clapper is visible below the rim of the bell. Have your child sit across the room from you. If you have more than one child, have them sit in a large circle. Atmosphere is important: the room should be darkened and still, the mood quietly dramatic.

Show the bell, drawing the children's attention to the clapper. Hold the bell with one hand, a little above waist level, arm comfortably bent but leading. Now, slowly and oh-so-carefully, begin walking toward your child. Exaggerate the care you are taking to keep the bell from ringing (remember, it will be much harder for him!). Keep your eyes on the bell. Standing in front of your child, signal him to stand and give him the bell carefully, without ringing it. Then return to sit while he carries the bell back to you or to someone else in the circle. Attention should be riveted on the clapper. The unintentional ringing of the bell provides instant feedback to the child to move more carefully. The child is reminded that he can, with a little effort, have more control over his movement.

Building Integrity

Would it be stretching the point to say that such simple exercises in the early years could prepare your children for more mature challenges later on?

Not really.

The child's first lessons in self-control are meant to give her a clear sense that she is master over one thing—her body. Later, she will extend that mastery to her plans, emotions, and even thoughts.

Think about it: as adults and parents, we are stewards over a lot. By contrast, our children begin with nothing but their own bodies. I challenge my own children by telling them clearly that their own bodies are the first thing given to them by God to learn to govern. When they are fidgety and restless, I remind them they are in control: "You are the boss of your own body. You can tell it what to do."

From their first words on, Tripp and I expect our children to use care in what they say and how they say it. Bad language, name-calling, sarcasm, or put-downs—none of that is tolerated whether they're six or sixteen. Because so much of this is typical TV sitcom stuff, sitcoms have always been off-limits in our family.

We teach our children that each person is precious to God and that our treatment of others should reflect this. Our expectations are high because we feel this is central to the harmony in our home.

As your children mature, they can and should be challenged to extend their control. For instance, in their reactions to life's frustrations, they need to learn that ending up with an extra buttonhole at the neck is not cause for a major meltdown but simply a signal to unbutton and rebutton the shirt properly.

To teach them well, as in the other areas, you need to model the appropriate behaviors. This means treating others (including your children) with kindness and learning to handle stress with graciousness. Isn't it interesting how helping our children realize their potential begins to help us realize our own?

Perhaps the finest area of self-control, comparable to the most refined motor skill, would be the control of our thoughts. I'm not speaking of repressing emotions but of learning how to think constructively and positively, of allowing God to use all things for good. You can begin early with your children to steer them away from feelings of victimization or blame of others. You can sympathize with their trials while teaching them to take responsibility for their responses. Above all, you need to discourage your children from making excuses for unacceptable behavior.

When society lowers its expectations, murmuring, "After all, they're only kids," a pattern is established of making excuses. Then we end up with condoms being handed out in high schools, backed by a pathetic "They're only teenagers. How can we expect them to be abstinent?" As mommies, we can begin to bring up our children with a higher standard.

The seeds of self-control need to be watered early to produce what they were meant to produce: responsibility, integrity, self-government, and self-esteem. We want our children to experience lives well lived, lives with no excuses. Begin by preparing them when they are young.

Concentration: "Quiet! Mind at Work!"

Pausing on her way to the laundry room, Diane gave three-year-old Gabriella an encouraging pat.

"I'm so glad you like those new sewing cards," she said, smiling.

Diane had found the set while exploring a nearby teachers' store and had finally found time to show them to Gabby yesterday. With only a few minutes before dinner, they'd had time to "sew" only one card together. Then back to the shelf it went.

This morning, after breakfast, Gabby had made a beeline for the sewing cards. She had chosen the orange lace and was carefully looping it through the holes around the yellow fish. Now she looked up and smiled briefly at her mom, then returned, absorbed, to her "sewing." Diane watched silently for a few minutes, ready to help Gabby fine-tune her efforts if necessary. But Gabby was doing well on her own, so Diane left. Mounds of laundry beckoned.

Doesn't the laundry always take longer than you think? A considerable chunk of time had passed before Diane emerged from the laundry room. *Better check on Gabby*, she thought. The now-completed orange-bordered yellow fish was prominently displayed on the table. Gabby had begun a blue flower with a purple lace.

Throughout the morning, as Diane finished each of her own chores, she returned to check on Gabby's progress. Most of the time, Gabby barely noticed her mother's presence. It seemed that the longer she "sewed," the more absorbed she became.

Finally all the cards were finished for Mom to admire. "Here, let's put them on the counter for Daddy to see when he comes home," Diane said.

"But, Mommy, can't I do them again?"

"Well, what about some of the other things on your shelves? How about a puzzle?"

Diane couldn't believe that Gabby, who'd already spent more than an hour with the sewing cards, would want to do them again. But Gabby was determined. Only after redoing the whole set did she turn to something else.

The next morning, when Gabby headed straight for the sewing cards, her mother tried to steer her toward something new, again without success.

"What's going on?" she asked me when she called. "Is it really okay for her to be so fixated on one thing?"

How Children Learn

It's not just okay, it's really good for children to focus so intensely and for long periods of time. This can mean they're building up their ability to concentrate, and that means they'll be better focused, more enthusiastic learners.

I love to catch one of my children lost in doing something they love. I may not be sure what the lesson is, but if a child is concentrating, I can be sure something is being built into him that will help him in the future, though it may be simply the ability to focus and concentrate.

The sensitive period for concentration occurs during the toddler years. It's a quiet drive rather than a powerful one. If independence is like a rushing river sweeping away everything in its path, concentration is more like a meandering brook. Not really concerned with getting where it's going, it follows an indirect path, picking up water from other sources and gaining momentum until it becomes a dependable, consistent stream. Here, obstacles must be removed and logjams broken to prevent the flow from being hindered.

Translated into practical terms, we need to help our children develop concentration by removing distractions and encouraging its growth into a strong and vital current.

You have already seen concentration in your child. Remember how your baby focused on the mobile above her crib or changing table even before she could touch it? Think of how she followed it with her eyes, concentration straining her whole body toward the bright objects above.

Remember when she found her hand? Remember how she held it at arm's distance and studied it for endless moments of baby time? How long could an adult hold his arm up in the air without tiring, even if he could experience the same sort of fascination with his fingers?

That's how a child's concentration is. It's spontaneous and surprising. It's not something you can make happen, but it is something you stumble upon. Once you discover it, you'll want to remember where to find it, though, because you want to encourage your child to spend as much time as she can there, bringing out the intense focus she showed when she discovered her own hand.

Give Choices

You can't force a child to concentrate, but you can maximize his opportunities. By observing and knowing your child well, you can learn what activities bring out the focus in him. When he chooses those things spontaneously, be supportive. When he needs help finding something to do, remember to offer options that have focused his attention in the past.

In the preschool years, it's especially important for children to choose their own activities. In the example of Gabby and her mom, Gabby was on the right track, choosing her own work rather than depending on her mother for direction.

Choice is also obviously linked with independence, but I bring it up here for a very specific reason: when the child chooses his own work, it is more likely he will bring his full attention to it.

Practice the Silence Game

This is an exercise in concentration, and a powerful spiritual lesson as well. Here's what you do:

- Gather your children to create the most quiet place possible.
- Turn off the phone and draw the blinds or curtains.
- Tiptoe and whisper.
- Sit cross-legged on the floor, leaving space around each person.
- Now, pour on the drama, letting your voice drop to the smallest whisper as you tell them how the game is played. By the end, your children should be using their utmost powers of concentration to hear you. "We're going to play the Silence Game. I'm going to tiptoe very quietly into the kitchen. You should close your eyes and listen very carefully. You'll need to hold your body perfectly still to hear me. I'm going to whisper your name. When you hear me whisper, come out without a sound. Remember, I'm going to whisper so quietly you can hardly hear me."
- After the last barely audible words, silently leave. Pause. From the next room, whisper the names of each of your children, starting with the ones least likely to hold still.
- Waiting for your parent's whisper as a child is a lot like the stillness we need later on to discern any impression our heavenly Father might want to make on our hearts. The Silence Game is early preparation for that stillness.

You can cultivate the ability to choose from the earliest years. Even before your child can dress himself, give him a choice between a blue shirt and a red shirt. As he begins to catch on, he can graduate to three or four choices. At some point—ideally, by the time he has learned to dress himself—he will become capable of choosing from all his own clothes. Help make that possible by making sure his dresser drawers are the right height and easy to open. Bring his closet rack down to his level.

Find ways to let him choose the order in which to do things: "Do you want to take your bath or brush your teeth first?" "The cat had her kittens; whom should we call first—Grandma or Daddy at work?"

By cultivating choice as part of his everyday life, you will teach your child how to exercise his will within appropriate limits. Before he even begins school, you should see the results: a child who chooses his own work and works independently. And remember, for all the reasons we mentioned before, this is most likely the child who will also be able to concentrate.

Encourage Repetition

A child who repeats activities is exhibiting strong concentration. Gabby's eagerness to lace the sewing cards again and again gave solid indication that she had great potential for learning. She might as well have been wearing a big sign that said: Quiet! Mind at Work!

Once Diane understood this concept, she saw her daughter's activities from a different perspective. She realized that along with encouraging Gabby to choose her activities, she could help her daughter further by allowing her to spend as much time as she wanted concentrating on one particular thing.

Repetition is always something to encourage; it helps the child develop his potential for concentration. It also means learning is taking place. So, for example, when your child finishes a puzzle, before scooping it up and putting it away, ask if he would like to do it again. If he has stacked a tower of nesting cups, ask if he would like to mix them up and build again.

Contrary to what we might assume in our often hectic society, a child who spends all morning on one or two activities is showing more learning potential than one who flits from one activity to the next. Do all you can to encourage your child to slow down and stick with something for a while.

Find the Window

Also closely tied with concentration is self-control, for a child who can't sit still will have a hard time focusing on anything. There is a saying, "Bring the body, and the mind will follow," which means that by disciplining our outer actions, we gain control of our thoughts and emotions. The exercises introduced in the previous section, walking on a line or walking with a bell, serve not only to perfect your child's self-control but also to sharpen his concentration skills.

Even the bounciest child will have at least one thing that will open the window of concentration. I know because I have one of the most in-motion children in the world! In addition to blessing me in many other ways, in her younger years Sophia took me to the limit of my assumptions about children. But even Sophia finally succumbed to something that released her potential to concentrate: coloring books.

Many years ago, I misunderstood coloring books; I never had them in the house. When my first two daughters received them as gifts, I threw them away. As a zealous, protective young mother, I was just certain that coloring in the lines would destroy my children's creativity.

I know better now. It would take much more than a mere coloring book to stifle the creative impulse of a young child. And I've learned that coloring books have definite merit. In addition to helping perfect fine motor control, they have an almost unequaled power to captivate the complete attention of even the most distractible child.

And so, when I found Sophia for the first time poised over the pages of a coloring book, oblivious to the comings and goings of the rest of our larger-than-life family, I think I hollered, "Hallelujah!"

Sophia's now fifteen and an excellent student who can actually sit still, but I think it all began the first time she picked up a marker and tried to stay inside the lines. Now she can concentrate on all the more complicated things required of her.

Use Challenging Activities

Concentration is a portable skill. Once the child's ability to concentrate has been evoked through one activity, she's better able to focus on others. That's why it's so important that when she finds something that absorbs her interest, you allow her to focus on that activity.

In addition to observing those unique activities that release your child's concentration, you can also use routine activities to challenge her.

For instance, show her in slow and exaggerated detail how to close a door without a sound. Show how turning the knob brings the latch in, how it is possible to hold the knob in such a way so as to release the latch only when the door is completely closed. Ask her to take a turn. Challenge her to carry a chair or stool across the room and set it down, again without a sound. With the utmost concentration, setting down one leg at a time, it is possible.

This distinction between sound and silence is a great place to sharpen your child's powers of concentration. Sit together with eyes closed (the better to concentrate) and list the noises you hear. In the most quiet room of your house (uncarpeted), show her a pin and ask her to close her eyes and tell you when she hears it drop.

As you begin to observe your child concentrating and watch her potential develop, you'll develop a deeper appreciation for the role concentration will play in her life now and later on.

Concentration is a necessity for your child's ability to learn—an invaluable key that will unlock many doors of opportunity. The child who can concentrate, who can focus completely, who can devote himself completely to a task, will thrive in an academic environment. As an adult, he will be able to bring his best to any task and therefore be better equipped to make a significant contribution.

Concentration counts—don't let your child leave home without it.

Part 2

Measures

Man looks at the outward appearance, but the LORD looks at the heart.

1 Samuel 16:7

The Keys to Gracious Service

One of my most frequent prayers is that I could actually read more than a couple pages before falling asleep at night. I know I'm barely getting anywhere when Tripp starts to close the pages of the book that's fallen by my pillow and I wake suddenly, mumbling, "I'm still reading."

Then, as I rummage through the pages to find my place I realize I don't even remember where I was anyway.

Exhausted mommies: it's a hard-knock life for us.

Which is why way back when I began planning this book—which wouldn't deal with just one aspect of motherhood but the whole enchilada as far as I've been able to figure it out to date—I wanted to make it easy. To make it more interesting and memorable for too-tired-to-remember-much mommies, I fell into three rhyming parts: Treasures, Measures, Pleasures.

The first and last parts made obvious sense. Treasures—that is finding out what our kids are all about, the natural resources

God has stored inside each one. Pleasures—that is having fun and getting more out of family living.

But Measures? Was I stretching just a little to come up with a convenient rhyme scheme?

I wanted to know, because in between discovering our kids as treasures and sharing life's pleasures with them is a part of parenting very dear to my heart: building a strong work ethic and good character. To me, these flowed naturally from trying to provide for the sensitive periods and the spiritual needs of our children.

As a mom who's still raising little ones, I've been blessed to see in my grown-up kids that every thought Tripp and I gave to the process, every discussion we had, every attempt we made to improve our parenting skills, and every sacrifice eventually paid off with great rewards. To tell you the truth, as an older mother who's often wiped out well before the end of the day, I find my older children to be incentives that keep me going when I might otherwise be too pooped to pop. Not to mention all the help they provide when they're home.

Tripp and I never took a casual approach to parenting. Because both of us had dads who abandoned their families and working mothers with alcohol problems and a laissez-faire approach to morality, we knew that once we decided we wanted to raise a wholesome, healthy family, we had to put a lot of thought into how to go about it.

Some mommies reading this may have had good role models. You're that much ahead. But some may be starting from scratch like we did. You need to know that if you didn't have a happy childhood, you can have the next best thing—creating one for your own kids. And I can promise you, there's a lot of healing in the process.

No matter what your background, you can build a healthy, happy, wholesome family. But it doesn't happen by accident. You have to spend some time planning how to go about it.

I call this "intentional parenting." By that I mean not just fa-la-la-ing along from day to day, assuming that attending church, school, and Little League will be enough to produce the kind of men and women our culture needs—children we will be proud of and enjoy spending time with when they're grown. I mean thinking long-term, taking our responsibility seriously (though it's important to have fun, which we'll spend time on in part 3), and correcting our course if we're not headed in the right direction.

Sometimes just grabbing hold of a very small idea can mean big changes for your family and your children's future. My prayer, of course, is that *The Mommy Manual* will be chockful of such ideas, and that you will feel equipped and empowered to keep on keeping on with the important calling God has given you.

Remember, motherhood is more than a job. It's a calling. Though it's rarely given the status or honor it deserves in our society, I'm confident that to God it is one of the two most important callings around. The other being fatherhood.

If God has called you to motherhood, he knows you won't start out anywhere near perfect. Remember, he doesn't call the equipped, he equips the called. So your motherhood journey is bound to be filled with growth and change, not just on your kids' part but on yours. As you come across new bits and pieces of information that inspire you to do things differently, be careful not to beat up on yourself for any past mistakes, but simply acknowledge them, giving thanks for the opportunity to change.

Believe me, I've had those moments of realizing I've fallen short as a mother, and I know more than most that by God's grace all things are made new. Because I grew up without God and without much moral guidance, I made many mistakes and hurt many people before I found the truth, and the truth set me free. Now look at what God has done with me!

Wherever you are as a mother, rest assured God has big plans for your life—and he has big plans for your children as well.

This brings me back to Measures, and why I ended up thinking it was the perfect title for what I wanted to share about work ethic and character in part 2.

As I first thought about the word, it sounded somewhat Shakespearean—noble and challenging and a little old-fashioned. Still, not wanting to pound a square peg into a round hole, I hauled out my dictionary. There, among oodles of definitions, I found these two for *measure*, the noun:

- The extent, dimensions, capacity, etc., of anything.
- Any standard of valuation, comparison, and judgment.

And these two for the verb:

- To find out or estimate the extent, dimensions, etc.
- To choose or weigh carefully one's words or actions.

There are also these idioms:

- Measure up—to be considered according to some standard.
- Take measures—to take action; to do something to accomplish a purpose.
- Take someone's measure—make a judgment of someone's ability and character.

Still with me? While definitions are often dull, when I thought about these in relationship to children destined to grow into men or women, I found *measures* to be an effective word to use in conjunction with intentional parenting—the part that has to do with increasing my children's capacity to serve, building their abilities and character, enabling them to become all God created them with the potential to be.

The phrase "measure of a man" has been the title of numerous books, CDs (most recently, a Clay Aiken album), and songs. Looking up book summaries and song lyrics, I found a common theme running through everything with that title: that the true measure of a man (or woman) cannot be judged by outer circumstances, successes or failures, but by character and heart.

Yes I know we're dealing with little children, but I think—no, now that I've raised a few successfully, I know—that if we have a vision for where they're going, we will raise better men and women for the future.

By vision, I don't just mean starting a college fund. In fact, I think it's wrong to decide in advance that all of your children will go to college. What if God calls them to do something else? How can a family hear God's direction if the parents have already decided something eighteen years ahead of time?

What I'm really talking about is service and character. Because while I think it's wrong to plan our children's future education or occupation, I think it's very, very right to plan that they grow into kind, gracious, compassionate, and generous adults who think of others before themselves.

Small Beginnings: Love Made Visible

If you dropped by our house any morning, there'd be no doubt in your mind that we have a lot of children. Voices from every direction—the early birds cheerful, the sleepyheads grumbling as they track down wayward books and backpacks. Feet clumping, bottoms bumping down the stairs. Washer whooshing, kettle whistling, three-ring binders clicking shut. Cabinet doors opening to receive last night's dinner dishes and offer this morning's cereal bowls.

Just the usual controlled pandemonium as five kids prepare themselves, their breakfasts, and their lunches while juggling morning chores and extra help for the three youngest who still need it.

Wait a minute. Did I say morning chores? Taking care of the younger children? Maybe it sounds like quite enough—way beyond the norm—that the kids are taking care of themselves rather than relying on Mom. Is it possible to expect so much of children on a daily basis?

The secret every mom needs to know is this: it's not only possible to teach your children to help around the house, but it's absolutely essential to their development. Once you begin to use the keys to a good work ethic, you will see how instilling an attitude of teamwork among all family members will enrich each individual and the family as a whole.

Serving others is an integral part of the Christian life. We all start out as helpless, demanding, and self-centered little creatures. Growing up is all about learning to think beyond our own needs and desires and learning to meet those of others. But beyond just maturing, the gift of cheerful, selfless service is a spiritual distinctive that sets us apart and truly enables our light to shine.

Loving service is the example Christ set for us. I believe it is the key to true satisfaction in life.

But does this relate to toddlers? Absolutely. The desire to serve is a potential God has built into each of us. You see it in three-year-olds eager to do any kind of work they see their parents do. So why do younger children clamor to help while older children are often lazy and resentful?

We've seen it already, with independence, order, self-control, and concentration. Just as with the other sensitive periods, the desire to serve emerges and is strongest during the toddler years. For it to be released fully, it must be encouraged at the appropriate time, when it first begins. A child who is not given opportunities to serve early on will be the one who balks at serving when it is required later.

Unlike the other sensitive periods, which can be developed in a classroom setting, the seeds of service find their most fertile soil in the home. In the family, God has provided a unique training ground for this potential.

Even if you're reading this with your first baby still in your arms, it's not too early to be thinking of making service a priority. It's never too soon to develop a vision for your family. What kind of home do you want for your children? Is it really possible to raise children who think of others more than themselves? How can we get them started?

I remember four-year-old Jonny hauling a small trash basket down the hall. The moment stands out in my memory because though Jonny was four, since he has Down syndrome, at the time he was more like a two-year-old developmentally. But here he was, just like any other little child wanting to make his contribution to the family.

He was so proud of himself because he knew he had taken a big step. He'd often seen his brothers collecting the baskets to empty into the big container in the garage. And because Jonathan looks up to his brothers, he wanted to do it too.

Can you imagine what would have happened if, thinking him too young or too disabled, I had taken the basket and emptied it myself? Of course, I knew there was a chance he would spill the basket. But what was most important here was not efficiency but nurturing my son's desire to be of service—and the sense of joy every young child feels when he is useful.

The last thing a spontaneously helping child needs is an adult hovering and worrying over him. Instead, I had Zachary, then eight, get another full basket to accompany Jonny to the garage. There, the boys finished their mission together and then put the baskets away.

As our family got larger, it definitely became easier to instill a love of service, because the younger children have so many role models. Remember, your first child may one day be the oldest of a multitude; but whether she is the oldest of ten or two, what you have developed in her will set the tone and example for any who follow. Make sure you teach her well—she's a major investment in the future of all your children.

An only child especially needs to be encouraged to serve, to feel that his help is needed. This may take extra effort from parents who could easily do it all without their child's help.

As in so many areas of helping our children grow, the first challenge is ourselves. Perhaps we grew up with mothers who expected too little, who did everything for us. Some of us live in affluent communities where housekeepers, cleaning services, and lawn-care professionals abound. Or where parents just don't put much priority on kids helping at home.

If any of these are the case, this is one area where you need to go against the flow. Kids need to work—not so much because we need their help but for the sake of their own development.

I took my children on an international tour with the help of a stack of *National Geographic* magazines. Together we cut out pictures of children working all over the world, like the African girls walking back to their village with the day's catch, bearing a stack of shiny silver fish on their heads. Mexican children helping their mothers pound the corn to make tortillas. Children all over the globe sweeping huts, fetching water, hanging clothes to dry, toting younger siblings for busy parents.

In many countries, young boys learn their trades by their fathers' sides. Even in our own country, children growing up on ranches and farms help milk cows, shear sheep, bale hay, plant, and harvest.

But for most families in our country, the trend toward fewer children and more household conveniences has meant a decline in responsibility for children. In fact, people from other times and places might judge our children to be pampered and spoiled.

Perhaps we need to expect a little more?

Or maybe we just need to start looking at the children themselves and take our cue from them. Jonny carrying out the trash may have been a personal first, but it was only the most recent in a growing list of household chores he'd shown an interest in. And believe me, in our house, when someone shows an interest in a chore, it's theirs to keep—until a younger one comes along to take over.

In fact, in our family, as soon as you can stand, you can serve.

Toddlers love to help and feel honored to have something to do. Why not learn to think on their terms, to find ways to let them be useful? They need to know they are an important part of the family. Sometimes I wonder if a lot of crankiness in little children could be averted by making them feel less unimportant.

What, after all, can a toddler do? It doesn't come easily to most adults to turn things over to someone slower and less competent. At first, parents need a little reflection, careful planning, and patience to put some of these new ideas into practice.

Let's start with the obvious—housework.

The Power of a Push

Dr. Ruth Peters, a psychology contributor to NBC's *Today Show*, says: "Daily in my practice I see parents who have made the mistake of not taking the time and attention to teach their children to be workers and achievers. These kids have learned to settle for less rather than to face and challenge adversity, to become whiners rather than creative problem solvers, and to blame others for perceived slights and lack of success." But the ability to work hard, to tolerate frustration, and to take responsibility doesn't just happen without a push from parents.

Teamwork: Many Hands Make Light Work

At the doctor's office or the zoo, in grocery aisles or church parking lots, for years I've been answering questions. It starts with: "Are those all your children?" Then, no matter what direction the conversation has taken, it usually ends with the Big Question: "How do you manage?"

We figured things out gradually. After all, we started with one or two children ourselves. While it's no secret that big families have a high degree of efficiency, it's not necessarily a sign of anything other than the fact that we have to be efficient. Mothers of many—"grandmultiparas" in OB-GYN lingo—would be the first to admit we're not smarter, just responding to a desperate situation.

We're outnumbered.

Still, even the smallest family can use big-family techniques to make their own lives more manageable. At the same time you'll be nurturing your child's potential for service, which he can carry with him wherever he goes.

Children need to feel needed. And when it comes to the work necessary to manage a large household, they certainly are. In a smaller family, Mom might be able to do everything for everybody. But is that really what you want? Then not only would you be frustrated and tired, but you'd also be burdened with a houseful of spoiled children thinking only of themselves.

Look at your housework as belonging to all members of the family. Housework is something that has enormous benefits—I mean, don't you feel so much calmer when the house is cleaned up?—and should take as little time as possible.

Do the math with your kids: if one person cleans the house, it might take six hours, but if six of us work together, it will take only one. Which brings us to an answer more important than any quadratic equation: More Help from Kids = More Time with Mommy.

On housecleaning day, get everyone involved. I give my kids a chance to choose what they're going to do—"I'll vacuum upstairs," "I'll sweep and dust," "I'll clean the kitchen"—and then turn them loose. Only when they balk do I start giving assignments.

Organize everything with shared housework in mind. A stool in the laundry room means even the shortest family members can help fold clothes. Dishes on the bottom shelves enable a three-year-old to put away dishes or a four-year-old to set the table without help.

Keep cleaning supplies secure from roving toddlers; but once you've taught older children how to use them safely, make them accessible to those older children. Make them user-friendly. My kids always took more of a shine to cleaning the bathroom or washing the car when I put the essentials in a special rubber tote with a handle.

Especially if you have boys, be sure to watch Don Aslett's video *Is There Life after Housework?* (www.cleanreport.com). His techniques are a treasure, his humor is a breath of fresh air, and his enthusiasm is contagious. Besides, seeing a man as a housecleaning expert will add new appeal for the males of the house.

Ten-Minute Pickups

No, this isn't a health drink or aerobic exercise but a way of life at the Curtis house. Several times a day, whenever Mom feels that things are getting too crazy clutter-wise, she calls for a Ten-Minute Pickup. (Probably anyone could call for a pickup, but no one else seems to care as much as Mom.) This is our signal to drop what we're doing and look for things that need to be put away.

Sometimes she is desperate. Then she'll call for a twenty-minute pickup.

We work together, and soon everything is cleaned up. The little lines between Mom's eyebrows disappear. She says this is the key to her sanity.

God sure makes moms different, but it's worth whatever it takes to keep them happy.

the Curtis kids

What about Chore Charts?

What about chore charts? I can only offer my own experience. My wonderful husband once sought to improve our household routine by making a chore chart. It was an artful affair, a blue nubby flannel board with a clear vinyl pocket for each child, designed to hold chore cards he had prepared with calligraphy and stickers of vacuums, beds, dishes, brooms, etc. My job was to divvy up the cards each morning, checking later to make sure the children had done their work.

Sounds like just the thing a big family would need, doesn't it? But things aren't always as they seem. In our house the chore chart wreaked havoc. The children rapidly became territorial and argumentative about their chores ("Mo-om, I did the dishes yesterday!" "Why do I have more things to do?"). Besides the ugliness of their worrying about their share and what was fair, I also was spending more time in organization and follow-through.

We eventually took down the chore chart and went back to what had always worked. Score one for the old saying "If it works, don't fix it." What works for us is flexibility and spontaneity. What works is when I can ask someone to do something that needs to be done without hearing, "But that's not on the chore chart!" What works is when my children respond to my requests by taking responsibility without a lot of fuss and comparison.

112

I Like Lists!

Lists, on the other hand, now those have really worked for me. I'm talking about spontaneous lists made from a template I keep in my computer files. The template has the usual jobs listed with underlined spaces to the left for the kids to check off. When it's time for everyone to go to work, I just delete the jobs that don't need doing that day, add any special ones, and print in some kind of large, amusing font.

I leave it up to the kids to divide the work.

Having the jobs down in writing means I don't have to remind or nag anyone about anything. It makes the kids feel more independent, and they enjoy the feeling we all get from checking stuff off a to-do list.

What works especially well now, since I have older kids, is to leave a chore list behind while I go to the grocery store. When I come home, the house is spic and span—my children actually seem to work to a higher standard when I'm not there.

Different methods work for different families. If the chart method works for you, then use it. If it doesn't work, don't be disappointed or hard on yourself. Whatever you do, don't use a chore chart if it becomes more of a burden than a blessing. Keep in mind the big picture.

Your goal is children with generous hearts, not crankadoodles (try that word to get your child out of a funk) constantly measuring who did what. Build this heart of service from the early years. As your children grow in competence and confidence, continue to introduce new skills. Our children, looking up to the next older, have a sense of "graduating" to the next level of chores. That's a powerful motivator.

But start early. Include your toddler on the cleanup team, even if so far your team is just Mom and Dad. Give him a dust cloth—it will keep him busy by your side, a far more valuable endeavor than dumping Cheerios on the floor in the kitchen!

Delegation: Four Questions

I didn't like divvying up the chore cards, but I do have four guidelines for how I distribute work as part of our daily routine. Actually, they are four questions you can ask yourself about anything that needs to be done.

Can He Do It Himself?

Is your child able to dress himself? Clean his room? Clean up his own place after breakfast? Then he should. This first question is related to independence, and though it does not mean you should be rigid (it is okay and part of role modeling to help others), the rule of thumb is this: if he can do it himself, let him.

Can Someone Younger Do It?

In an amazing display of toddler-size service, when they were two and three, Madeleine and Jonny began to take the plastic cups and saucers out of the dishwasher in the morning and put them away in the cabinets. Since then, I've become more and more confident with delegating chores, as long as we've taken the time to show the little ones how to do things properly.

Now, all dishes except glasses are on the lowest kitchen shelves next to the dishwasher. Justin, my four-year-old, loves to empty the bottom rack of the dishwasher each morning while someone older and tall enough to reach the glasses cabinet empties the top rack and seven-year-old Daniel puts away the silverware.

Seven Strategies That Build a Strong Work Ethic

1. Start early. Lay the groundwork early. When our three-year-olds beg to peel carrots or our four-year-olds plead to sweep the floor, our tendency is to say they're not ready. But teach them when they're eager and they'll be more likely to step up to the plate later on.

2. Accept what you get. When faced with less-than-perfect results, graciously praise the effort. For example, when your seven-year-old surprises you with clean windows, ignore the smudges and smears. "What hard work! I love to clean windows too. Next time let's do it together!"

3. Know your children. There's a difference between a five-year-old who doesn't know about washing the backs of plates and a ten-year-old who's slacking. One needs teaching, the other needs correction. Parents also need to know how to motivate each child. Young children are often motivated by verbal praise. Older children may need more: money or privileges.

4. Teach delayed gratification. Establish a pattern: we work, and then we play. "I know you want to play outside. Let's pick up all these blocks and fold the clothes and then we can go together." Or, "Let's get the house cleaned up and then we'll make some popcorn and watch a movie."

5. Equip them to earn. Through the years we've given our kids a base allowance, plus bonuses for work done well and cheerfully. We've also encouraged them to find other ways to earn money. These have included raising rats for pet stores, paper routes, and a wood-splitting business. What all these ventures had in common was that they took an enormous amount of time and energy—mine and their dad's! If your child wants to rake leaves, be ready to knock on doors with him. If she wants to walk dogs, help her place an ad in the paper. Be ready and willing to help your child start working, and you'll be amazed at the life lessons she'll learn.

6. Encourage volunteering. Today, volunteerism is trendy. Many schools require community work from students each semester. For Christian kids, volunteerism holds a special resonance, as it means following Jesus's command to love and serve. When your children are young, find ways to involve them in your own service projects. Let them help deliver a meal to a new mom or houseclean for an elderly friend. Pick up trash on your street or on the beach, visit convalescent homes, or pull weeds for a next-door neighbor.

7. Be a role model. So much of who our children turn out to be is a reflection not of what we try to pour into them but of what they see in us. It's not the big occasions our kids will remember most but the everyday stuff that revealed what their parents were really made of—how we handled frustration, whether we were on time and kept commitments, whether we served others with a smile or a frown.

Like all good things, building a strong work ethic in your child takes constant effort. But you'll know it's worth it when your child comes home from the first day of his first job looking tired and satisfied and grown-up and says something like my oldest son, Josh, said to me: "My boss said I did a good job, Mom. Thanks for everything."

Actually, a younger child could do these chores, but Justin and Daniel have Down syndrome (since Jonny's and Madeleine's birth, we've adopted three little guys with Down's) and so are developmentally delayed.

There are chores even the smallest can do. Don't ask your eight-year-old to bring a diaper for the baby if your three-year-old is around. The younger child will relish the opportunity to serve, and the older child is capable of more advanced assignments. For big cleanups and small, work is distributed according to one principle: delegate any task to the youngest capable of doing it.

Can It Be Done Differently?

You may have grown up with a mother who was so perfect she ironed the sheets. Or maybe she didn't iron the sheets, but your friend's mother did, and you wondered why your mother didn't. Anywhere along the line, you may have picked up some ideas of perfection that just aren't adding much to your life.

Ever hear the story about the young wife who argued with her husband each Thanksgiving because she cut the turkey in half to roast it? When he insisted that it wasn't necessary, she asked her mother why she'd grown up with Thanksgiving turkeys cut in half. Mom, who couldn't remember seeing a whole turkey in her own childhood, had to go to Grandma to find out why. Grandma was amazed at the legacy she had passed on. And so were her daughter and granddaughter when she told them that she'd always cut the turkey in half because her oven was too small and the turkey too big to cook the normal way. What doesn't fit in your oven? Are you doing things in ways that are unnecessary or too exacting for your family?

116

Does It Need to Be Done at All?

When my fifth child came along, I began streamlining what I thought was necessary. The process went something like this: "Do the dishes need to be hand-dried and put away immediately or can they air-dry overnight?" The must-do's that were dropped were evidently of such small consequence that I can't even remember the others. A writer writes best from experience, and this was mine: I wanted my house to look nice. I wanted a lot of children. Though not mutually exclusive desires, pursuing both created some tension. Resolving that tension involved some compromise. Reaching that compromise took some time.

The principle that housework belongs to the whole family was always a priority. And that involved compromise, as well. For example, if I want my nine-year-old to vacuum, I need to understand that his result—even when he works to the best of his ability—will not look the same as mine.

Keeping that in mind, you can make a decision in advance to receive each child's personal best as though it were the best. As in my own experience of folding the clothes, this may involve lowering your standards for the finished product. That's okay. I want to assure you, as I used to assure myself, that this is one of those rare instances in which lower expectations will actually serve to achieve a higher purpose.

But what about breaking things? Most of us grew up with the idea that breakables should be kept away from kids. On the contrary, I would encourage you—if your dishes are breakable—to allow your child the responsibility of setting the table and putting the dishes away anyway.

Consider: how can a child learn to treat things carefully if you give him only things made of plastic? By keeping breakables out of bounds, you send the message that you think he's bound to fail. On the other hand, when you teach a child how to and let him use certain beautiful but breakable objects, you show that he is worthy of your trust.

Prepare your child by handling things with exaggerated care yourself. Draw his attention to the challenge. Always use confident, encouraging words to remind your child to be careful.

Under these circumstances, will your children sometimes accidentally break things? Yes, once in a while. Do you ever break things? Yes, once in a while.

But breaking is immediate feedback of careless movement. A child who has been taught to be careful will certainly get the message. Breaking something is a reminder to be more careful in the future.

Your own challenge is to accept in advance the fact that things will break and to react with graciousness when they do. That gives your children a lesson in good manners. But I can promise that by using the principles illustrated here, you will be surprised at how seldom things will break in your home.

Housework: Age-Appropriate Chores

Mommies who have been doing everything themselves may gasp on first hearing of "age appropriate" chores: *A two-and-a-half-year-old peeling carrots? A five-year-old sweeping the floor?*

Hold that gasp. Your child's success at household chores—when the chores are introduced early—will give him a sense of accomplishment and make him feel like an important part of the family.

We give children chores not so much because we need their help (although some of us with big families definitely do!), but because it's good for them.

Doing Things Differently:
A Personal Example

Early in my motherhood, I began to notice that children have a tough time keeping clothes neatly folded in their drawers. For a while I was frustrated at the time I had wasted folding. Then it occurred to me that folding could be a much more informal affair than I had ever imagined.

This will explain my current, casual routine. As I empty the dryer, I quickly and just barely fold big items (jeans, T-shirts, pajamas) in stacks, one per child. The children periodically come and get their stacks to put away in their rooms. In the meantime, the small items of clean laundry—socks, underwear, napkins—accumulate in the laundry basket until it threatens to overflow. Just before it does, I call all the children, turn on some music, and dump the clothes onto the carpeted floor of my bedroom. They fold together until the basket is empty; then everyone puts everything away.

I use this chore as an example and share it in such detail to reveal how chores don't have to be done the way your mother did them or the way your neighbor does them; instead they can be tailored to your family, keeping your priorities in mind. With the laundry, my goal was to get a very large and very necessary job done without any unnecessary stress, while promoting the joy of serving together as a family.

My choice involved modifying my standards about how folded clothes should look. But it was a choice I made willingly. Since at the time I made this decision, nine of my children were under thirteen, most of them were not capable of folding to perfection. But, as I said, clothes in children's drawers never seem to stay folded for long. And I've noticed wrinkled T-shirts have a way of smoothing out when my boys put them on.

Keep in mind that modifying your standards is not always a sign of laziness but sometimes of intelligent decision making. When we lower our standards because circumstances defeat us or we feel weak, we don't feel good about the result. But when we evaluate the demands on our time, our children's capabilities, and our family's priorities, a decision to temporarily modify our standards in some area may actually be the most responsible path.

The important thing is to analyze each task, breaking it down into a sequence of actions, then presenting the sequence slowly and carefully to the child. For example, to be successful at peeling carrots without injuring himself, the child needs to know the peeler is sharp, that he should grasp the peeler firmly in his dominant hand with the carrot in the other, and peel away from himself. To help your child succeed at learning to sweep, try drawing a chalk circle the first few times so he gets the idea of sweeping into a pile—the circle will make the abstract concrete for him until he "gets" it.

Also remember that as long as your child has done his best, don't scold him for less-than-perfect results. Try to be content with what he's done, or at least wait until he's busy somewhere else before "fixing" everything the way you want it.

But do try to let go and relax. Your kids may remember you for your clean kitchen sink and tidy bathroom, but if cleanliness and tidiness were associated with a lot of stress, those might not be the kind of memories you'd like.

I've listed some chores that come to mind on page 122, but of course there are many more. Use your judgment. Each child has his own timetable, so ages are suggested and approximate. Ages given are on the early side; for boys, who mature more slowly, add six months to ages given.

By ten years old, a child should be able to learn any housekeeping skill, as long as you are willing to teach him. Certain skills, such as ironing, mowing the lawn, and babysitting for siblings depend on maturity level and/or family circumstances. Parents know best.

Hearts to Serve: Preparing Hearts and Minds

While you may decide to lower your expectations regarding the appearance of your house—or the folded clothes—I encourage you at the same time to set your expectations higher regarding your children's attitude toward serving others.

Here's another culture-based issue worth examining: our society values some types of work more highly than others. We think of janitorial work and trash collection as lowly work. And how many times have you heard "burger flippers" used as a derogatory remark, as in, "Do you want to be a burger flipper the rest of your life?"

Though this may be the way of the world, this is not the way of Christ.

When our Christian values are at odds with the world's, it's our responsibility as parents to weigh the difference and carefully consider how to pass on what is right to our children. In addition, our children need to see that we ourselves live out what we are teaching them.

My view is this: Jesus modeled a life of service. He gave everything, no holding back. He preached to thousands at the Sermon on the Mount, but he also washed his disciples' feet. This shows me that all service is pleasing to God, that he doesn't attach greater status to one form than another. More important than the service is the heart of the one who serves.

In practical terms, this means that changing a diaper—if done in the proper spirit—is as important as negotiating a peace treaty. If I want my children to have a Christlike attitude toward service, I begin by modeling it myself. This is one area where actions definitely do speak louder than words.

Prepare Your Heart

As in so many other aspects of being a parent, the first step in preparing your children's hearts for service is to prepare your own.

121

1 1/2 years:

Getting diaper for self or new baby

Putting disposable diaper in trash

Picking up small items from floor

Shutting cabinet doors

Turning on dishwasher

2 years:

Putting away toys

Emptying dishwasher—putting away plastic dishes and cups

2 1/2 years:

Folding napkins

Helping set table

Putting away silverware

Peeling carrots

Pouring measured items into mixing bowl

Putting away broom and dustpan

3 years:

Emptying dishwasher—putting away breakables

Dusting lower shelves

Emptying small trash cans

Carrying stacks of clothes to rooms

Dust-mopping hardwood floors

Participating in food preparation

4 years:

Feeding baby

Feeding pets

Putting away books

Further dusting

Sorting recyclables

Simple food preparation—peanut butter and jelly sandwiches, nachos

5 years:

Making bed

Setting table

General straightening of rooms

Sweeping

Folding laundry

Raking leaves

6 years:

Pouring milk for family meals

Clearing table

Emptying trash

Weeding

Washing lower windows

Polishing silver, brass

7 years:

Vacuuming

Loading dishwasher

Sweeping floor

Opening cans

Cleaning windows

Helping with grocery shopping

Sorting laundry

Shoveling snow

8 years:

Washing pans

Cleaning bathrooms

Cooking involving recipes

Sewing buttons

Helping with grocery list

9–10 years:

Loading washer and dryer, adding laundry products, choosing correct machine settings

Changing baby's diapers

Helping with meal planning

Further cooking skills

Washing car

Pray for God to show you the areas where your own attitude needs adjustment. When you find an attitude toward work that's robbing you of joy—perfectionism, balking, resentfulness—ask God to help you change. He will. And haven't you already been surprised at how much easier it is to change negative attitudes when you're thinking of your children?

Find the joy in your own daily work, so your children can find joy in what you ask them to do. Give your best, and they will give their best.

Use Biblical Examples

The New Testament is filled with stories of service, of those who gave from the heart: the Good Samaritan, Mary breaking the alabaster jar to anoint Jesus, Jesus himself giving all for us. Share these with your children from their earliest days. As your children grow, you'll be able to use these stories to show them how to apply biblical principles in their own lives.

From the time a child is born, his character is being formed. That's why the preschool years are so important. Many experts feel that by the time a child is ready for school, the kind of adult he will be is already determined. This doesn't mean a child can't change, but after the early years change occurs only through a concentrated application of the will. How much easier, when you think about it, to build the best into them from the beginning!

The toddler years have quite a reputation. They are, after all, where we see the most pure and unashamed self-centeredness. And yet we see that God has built into each of us, like an antidote to the disease, the potential to serve. I see it when even my youngest wants to help me fold the clothes or wash the dishes or put away the groceries.

A Spoonful of Scripture

As a nanny, Mary Poppins got her young charges working with a bouncy song about a spoonful of sugar helping the medicine go down. I highly recommend teaching that one to your children, as well as "Just Whistle While You Work" from Disney's *Snow White and the Seven Dwarves*. The Bible also gives us some good advice about serving others:

"Two are better than one, because they have a good return for their work" (Eccles. 4:9).

"Commit to the LORD whatever you do, and your plans will succeed" (Prov. 16:3).

"Even a child is known by his actions, by whether his conduct is pure and right" (Prov. 20:11).

"He who works his land will have abundant food, but the one who chases fantasies will have his fill of poverty" (Prov. 28:19).

"Whatever you do, work at it with all your heart, as working for the Lord, not for men" (Col. 3:23).

"Serve one another in love" (Gal. 5:13).

"If anyone serves, he should do it with the strength God provides, so that in all things God may be praised through Jesus Christ" (1 Peter 4:11).

The potential for serving others might be eclipsed by the desire to please ourselves were it not for Jesus, who showed us the way to triumph over sin, over selfishness. Your task as a parent is to give that gift to your children. The lessons begin in the early years in the home, but they will extend later into the life of the children in school, in church, and in the community. It is one thing to teach your children the Golden Rule: "Do unto others as you would have them do unto you." But the Golden Rule will remain only a concept until it has been actively applied. Opportunities to serve—especially when they involve helping those who are helpless (older children diapering babies or tying toddlers' shoes)—engrave the Golden Rule on your child's heart. And a child who lives the

Golden Rule will extend the lessons beyond service and into more refined areas of manners, charity, and hospitality.

And who needs to worry about self-esteem, now a major preoccupation among worldly educators? A child who grows up with a healthy attitude toward service will be competent and confident. In my estimation, ten minutes helping Mom and feeling appreciated will build more self-esteem than a week of watching Barney!

Unselfishness: The Nature of Service

My daughter Jasmine was born six years after her older sister, Samantha. For seven years Jasmine was the baby of the family. At seven, she became the middle child when her brother Joshua was born. Then, abruptly, our family pattern changed with child after child born eighteen months apart. When Samantha married, Jasmine officially became the oldest child. For years our dinner table looked like Snow White and the seven, eight, and finally nine dwarves.

Because of her family, Jasmine had to work harder than most kids her age. But she did it with good humor and grace. She was able to do it well because she embraced her life and was grateful for the family God chose to place her in.

Today, Jasmine is a wonderful wife and mother with four little ones of her own—God rewarded her and then some. That might

---

Jasmine's Secret to a Happy Life

"If you want to be treated like a servant, act like a princess. If you want to be treated like a princess, act like a servant."

My daughter was only eleven when she formulated her plan for successful living. She'd already learned from her own experience what had been written long ago: "A generous man will prosper; he who refreshes others will himself be refreshed" (Prov. 11:25).

125

not have been the outcome had she chosen a different path, had she become bitter or longed for a more "normal" lifestyle.

Her embrace of the life God had placed her in was a beautiful example. As a teenager, she arrived at a spiritual maturity many adults never experience, understanding that in giving so much, she was truly the one who gained.

4

The Keys to Gracious Character

Long ago, when I was a D.C. latchkey kid, my mother would leave a couple dollars and a list for me to go to the store after school. I'd walk down New Hampshire Avenue to "our" grocery store, load a basket, cross my fingers I'd have enough money not to have to put anything back, then carry my bounty home in a double brown bag.

Forty years later I shop in a suburban megamarket forty times larger than that humble store. Between leaving my empty van and returning to fill it with our family's food supply I walk at least a mile, browsing aisles brimming with an assortment of food fit for a king: a dozen apple varieties, a hundred imported cheeses, scores of pasta possibilities, frozen foods galore, an astonishing assortment of breads, and an ever-more-outrageous array of ice creams.

Okay, so I'm an older mother. I don't mean to come across like a caricature "Yesiree, back in my day we walked three miles to school with holes in our shoes," but surely even the youngest mothers have noticed that the world their kids are growing up in is just not the same as it was even when they were kids—and it seems to be changing ever more rapidly.

I guess it would be scary if our children didn't seem so downright competent to handle it all. I remember the black-and-white TVs we'd circle round to watch *The Ed Sullivan Show* and *I Love Lucy*. Each set had four knobs—the off/on/volume control, brightness, horizontal hold, and vertical hold (because for some reason, picture stability was very fragile, and out of the blue, the picture on the screen would start flipping up or down or sideways—we've come a long way, baby!).

Pretty straightforward, and yet our parents never let us touch the knobs, so sure we'd break the TV. Now my fifth-grader's doing Power Point presentations and I'm trying to schedule an appointment for her to teach me. I don't worry when a new techno-marvel makes its entrance into our house, because any of my children can probably figure it out for me.

See what I mean? We have so many reasons to be confident about the ability of the next generation to cope with rapid change and technology.

Still, I worry. Do you?

Because it takes more than competence, intelligence, or education to produce the kind of man or woman I want each of my children to grow up to be.

There's a word that comes to mind here: *mensch*. It's one of those Yiddish words (Yiddish is a Germanic language written in Hebrew and includes many special Hebrew words, especially those that have to do with faith). *Mensch* is a challenge to translate, but because it means exactly what I'm talking about here, I'll try.

128

The German language has the word *mann* for *man*. But *mensch* means so much more. One dictionary defines *mensch* as "a person having admirable characteristics, such as fortitude and firmness of purpose." *Mensch* also signifies a perfect gentleman or a perfect lady, someone compassionate, caring, and kind.

So when I think about the kind of adults I want my children to grow up to be, I'm thinking menschen—men and women with good, strong, and gracious character. I want them to grow up to be faithful wives and husbands, loving parents, brave believers, good friends, and committed citizens.

Over the years, my kids have been educated at home, in public, Catholic, and Christian schools—it's a decision I make year by year, child by child. But no matter where they receive their academic education, their dad and I are well aware that their character development is our responsibility.

Your child may have Sunday school, VBS, and even schoolteachers who are committed to her spiritual well-being and actions in the world. But no one will have the impact on your child that you do. It's really kind of exciting to think what important work lies before us in shaping the next generation and the future, one child at a time.

And we need to get an early start. For just as in the other areas of children's learning, the best foundation is laid early on, values and virtues are more likely to stick, to be part of who the child really is, if they are part of her early experience.

But they need to be introduced on the child's terms, in ways compatible with the young child's learning style.

Remember, children under eight are not abstract thinkers. Words like *courage* and *perseverance* cannot be understood by themselves but can become part of the child's value system through stories and talks about everyday situations and how to handle them.

Tripp and I have already seen the tremendous impact of this early exposure, because some of our kids are on the tail end of this process—Samantha and Jasmine are raising families of their own, Josh and Matt are living independently, and Ben is in college. At home, Zach and Sophia are in high school, Maddy and Jonny are in sixth grade, and Jesse, Daniel, and Justin are bringing up the rear.

Through all those growing up years, I've met a lot of other parents and seen a lot of parenting styles, from what I call barn-cat parenting (no plan for the future, no clue what's going on) to laissez-faire parenting (no plan, some clue) to flying-by-the-seat-of-our-pants parenting (some plan, no clue) to intentional parenting (made a plan and caught a clue).

One of the saddest things I've seen is kids growing up with faith and values who drop everything they've been taught when they get to their teens. A 2002 study by the Southern Baptist Convention's Council on Family Life found that 88 percent of evangelical children leave the church soon after high school graduation. Based on my own observation of families through the years, I think a lot of the reason is this: just as most parents (rightly or wrongly) delegate their children's academic education to schools, they also expect church/Sunday school/Bible studies to see to their spiritual and character development.

No way.

Our children need to hear from our own lips the things that matter most. They need to see it lived out in our own lives. They need to learn how to discern God taking care of them as they find their place in the world.

Values and virtues—the things of the spirit—do not exist in a vacuum. It's up to us to demonstrate to our children just how vital values are in our daily lives.

Snuggle-Up Lesson

If a picture's worth a thousand words, a movie's worth a million. And because movies involve more senses, they have an even greater impact on children.

One of the blessings of videos is that they bring other cultures right into our living rooms, a powerful way to teach a spiritual lesson. Try a gem of a tale like *Children of Heaven*, nominated for an Academy Award as best foreign film of 1997. Set in Iran, it is a simple story of a boy who picks up his sister's newly repaired shoes, then misplaces them while running the rest of the family's errands. Both of the children are anguished by the loss, as each has only one pair of shoes. They dare not tell their parents, who are already behind in rent and struggling to keep food on the table. And so they come up with a plan to share the brother's shoes. How they manage, and how eventually the brother finds a way to earn another pair of shoes, paints a portrait of selfless love, steadfastness, and grace.

All the easier for children to absorb when the main characters are children and the problem is child-sized. What young viewer could ever look inside his own closet—or at his own brothers and sisters—in the same way again?

Granted, some kids turn out okay no matter how uninvolved their parents. But why take chances? If you want to maximize your child's chances of success—and by success, I mean growing into a mensch—you need to be intentional, you need to have a plan, and you need to stay clued in to your child through every step on the road to maturity.

Gratitude: In All Things, Thanks

When I mentioned going to the grocery store and hoping I'd have enough money to pay for all the groceries on the list, I wasn't kidding. There were many times in my childhood when

Building an Attitude of Gratitude

It's hard to go wrong when your heart is giving thanks. Here's how:

Acquaint your children with God as provider. Teach them that food, clothing, and home come not from you but through you—from God.

Play tapes of praise and thanksgiving in the car and during housework.

Find ways to be grateful even for chores; for example, setting the table reminds us that by God's grace we are fed. Why wait till grace to thank him?

Model gratitude for your children by sharing all that God has done for you, especially the small things.

I had to put a few things back because there just wasn't enough to pay for everything we needed. There were times my brothers and I ate oatmeal for dinner the last few days before my mother's paycheck.

And there was a time or two we didn't eat at all.

I'm actually grateful for that experience. Grateful that my house and my clothes weren't as nice as those of my classmates. Grateful I couldn't always have what I wanted. I wrote a lot about this in my book *Lord, Please Meet Me in the Laundry Room*, trying to convey how the memory of those early years makes it impossible for me to take for granted my life today.

You might say I'm grateful for my past because it taught me to be grateful for my present.

But how to communicate that to my kids, who live in what I can only describe as a culture of plenty? Because no matter how strapped for cash a family might be—and ours is definitely there sometimes—we still have so much more materially than poor or even average families had two generations ago.

The cultural circumstances in which kids grow up have an enormous impact on shaping the character of the entire generation. That's why those who grew up in the Great Depression are so cautious with money and concerned with thrift. One sixty-something lady I know saves every bit of paper and string, even washes out her sandwich bags to reuse them.

Kids growing up today are in danger of living at another extreme—wasteful and ungrateful. They're prone to say they're starving at the first twinges of hunger, ask for Super Size, then leave food on their plates. Some think they have nothing to wear when their closets are full of clothes, or say they're bored rather than recognizing the multitude of options available to them.

It almost makes you wonder if their lives would be improved if times were just a little tougher. I mean, I'm thankful Tripp and I are able to give our children so much that I missed, but I'm also uncomfortably aware of how those advantages crowd out the character building that comes from never being able to take your school clothes, your medicine, or even your next meal for granted.

We have so much to be grateful for. My teens and I love to watch the old *Honeymooners* show with Jackie Gleason, but I've wondered aloud with them how they would feel about living in Ralph and Alice's teensy, decrepit apartment. And what about those first suburban housing developments that spread the blessing of single-family home ownership after World War II? Did you know that since the very first Levittown home was built, the average square footage for American homes has almost doubled?

And remember when eating out was a rare treat?

So what does this have to do with raising little children? Or do you already see where I'm going with this? It's something I've thought carefully about for many years: while children from what we call "underprivileged" backgrounds need a little extra help to reach their potential, children from privileged backgrounds have some special needs of their own, needs that must be met if they are to grow up to be caring, compassionate, and kind.

I chose gratitude as the first key to gracious character because it seems to me that everything else flows out of it: if my children

Sending the Message without Words

I can do a lot of talking about my life and reminding my kids what I expect from them (where two or more are gathered, there Mama will give a sermon!) or I can find ways to reach them that are better suited to their needs—and more effective too.

I begin early on introducing my children to other cultures. There are so many reasons why this is a good idea, but one in particular is this: since people in many parts of the world do not have access to an abundance of food or adequate housing, seeing pictures of daily life in other parts of the world brings a message without words but with a lot of power.

Keep in mind that children learn differently than we do. Young children under age six are not at all capable of abstract thinking. But concepts can be communicated through pictures and stories.

I've found *National Geographic* to be a wonderful resource. You can access back issues online, but I prefer the magazine for a more multisensory approach. You can subscribe or pick up old copies at garage or library sales.

Sometimes, I'll gather up my kids and a stack of *Geographic*s and suggest, for example, that we hunt for pictures of shelters, explaining that some people don't have houses but tents or huts. Or we might look for pictures of people dancing or mommies with children.

As we discuss the pictures, it's nice to have a globe handy to show them where the countries are. When we have a collection of pictures, we glue them on a poster board, adding a Bible verse that sounds appropriate for the subject.

Lately I've taken to laminating and hanging pictures of children in faraway places at my children's eye level—like one picture of an overcrowded, rundown African classroom stuffed with children eager to learn. Or a too-thin boy with a torn and ragged shirt looking straight through the camera lens into our hearts.

Rather than commenting on the pictures or pointing out the difference in circumstances, I pray that the Holy Spirit might inspire my children with gratitude for what they have and a greater willingness to share.

are grateful, it will be easier for them to be respectful, honest, compassionate, and generous.

What I mean is that our children can honor and obey us because the Bible tells them they have to or they can honor and obey because they are grateful for the parents God gave them. A husband and wife may honor their vows out of obedience or they may honor them giving thanks to God for their marriage. A student may do his homework to avoid bad grades or he may strive for the best because he is grateful for his education.

The Greek philosopher Cicero came to the same conclusion long before me, writing in 54 BC: "Gratitude is not only the greatest of virtues, but the parent of all others."

Respect: Someone to Watch over Me

When respect flows out of gratitude, then it's authentic, then it's real—and isn't that how you want it to be for your children? You want their respect for you to be based not on fear but on a true appreciation of God as their provider, and Mommy and Daddy as the parents God has provided.

There's really nothing quite so ugly as a young child, or any child, for that matter, speaking scornfully to her mom, something I saw recently while talking to another mother at a school fair. Barging abruptly into our conversation, the second-grader held out her hand and demanded money with a belligerent why-haven't-you-already-given-it-to-me attitude. The mother, completely cowed, fumbled in her purse and forked over a few dollars with a sheepish apology to her very obnoxious little girl.

Heaven help these two! was all I could think, as this mother-daughter duo was only eight years into their relationship and it was already going so badly. At what point had her baby's adoring gaze morphed into contempt? How had an eight-year-old developed the upper hand in their relationship? And didn't this mother respect herself enough to expect more from her child?

I know this is an extreme case, but it underscores the absolute necessity of respect for parents. The mother/child relationship is an important anchor in the child's identity and relationship to the world. If you want your child to respect himself and to respect others, then he must carry forward from his infantile adoration a loving appreciation and deep respect for Mommy.

It's not as simple as "Seven Easy Steps to Respect." Because there's something mysterious about respect—certain people command respect just by their presence. Think how some teachers have better control of their classes than others—even the same group of kids can behave differently for different adults.

Here is what I think is going on: kids "read" adults, intuitively picking up on inner weaknesses and self-doubt. And so it comes down quite simply to this: a mommy with healthy self-esteem, quiet confidence, and a sense that she deserves respect will receive it from her children.

Does that mean a child will never slip up and act or speak disrespectfully? I think every child at some point sees how far she can get with challenging authority. But any incident of disrespect needs to be confronted on the spot, with the goal of making it the last.

In so many areas these days, our culture shrugs its shoulders and says, "Kids will be kids." Some parents think it's only natural for kids to sass their parents. I disagree. We teach our children to wear seat belts. We teach our children not to smoke or do drugs. We certainly can teach them to be respectful.

I don't allow my children any leeway in this area and have been known to say, "You don't have to like me, but you do have to respect me." If my children like me, that's icing on the cake—but I can't teach them anything or have any influence over their lives if they begin to go down the road of disrespect.

It's not for my benefit. It's so I can do the job God gave me to do of raising and guiding them. It's for their sake that respect is important. For in another mysterious way, their own self-respect is based on their ability to respect their mom, their dad, their family.

Respect generalizes like that. A truly respectful person, not one just playing by the rules but one whose attitude of gratitude gives them a deeper understanding of how we all fit into God's plan, treats everyone, *everyone*, with graciousness.

This is what I want for my children. And one thing Tripp and I did to create a home based on respect was to ditch television.

The reason was simple: we didn't like the sitcoms that were nightly fare on the major networks. Even more offensive than the preoccupation with sex and the crude humor, the putdowns and sarcastic dialogue set a bad example for children. If that seems a little over the top, just remember that companies spend millions to advertise products because TV has tremendous influence.

We wanted to bypass that influence, and we made this decision early on because I just did not want to be sitting at the dinner table listening to a bunch of bickering, smart-alecky teenagers.

Later, when satellite reception offered a greater variety of channels, we jumped at the opportunity. We were homeschooling then, and the availability of history, science, and arts programs made satellite irresistible. But we blocked MTV and just established a pattern with our children of bypassing network shows and seeking out more intelligent fare.

This is a radical approach, I know. I'm not suggesting it for every family. And I'm not sharing it from any feelings of self-righteousness. It was just a decision I made because I thought it would support my intentions for my children—that they would grow up to be gracious, respectful, and kind to their parents, teachers, brothers, sisters, and friends.

In addition to self-respect and respect for family and friends, I wanted my children to be respectful of all races, cultures, classes, and occupations. A lot of what I discussed in the previous chapter has helped with that, as I've tried to help my children understand that there are other factors besides surroundings and material possessions that give every individual in every culture his or her own unique dignity. We need to try to see things through God's perspective: "The LORD does not look at the things man looks at. Man looks at the outward appearance, but the LORD looks at the heart" (1 Sam. 16:7).

That's a verse Jonny's kindergarten teacher used when writing to me about how having my son with Down syndrome in her class had changed her and the children's lives forever. Kids take their cues from the adults around them. All God's creatures, no matter their mental or physical abilities, are worthy of respect.

As I mentioned before, I cringe when people use the term "burger flipper" in a scornful way. It's not our work that defines who we are, but our attitude. Therefore, the school janitor is as worthy of my child's respect as the school principal. Both are there to serve. God loves them the same.

The model I aspire to and want my children to aspire to is this: to not behave one way with one person and another way with someone else because of wealth, position, or power, but to treat all people respectfully based on the fact that we are all the same in God's eyes.

Accountability: Truth Sets Us Free

Through the ages, all sorts of grown-ups have had all sorts of ideas about the state of the child's soul. Some philosophers have thought children were born innocent and pure and that any inclination toward evil had to be generated from outer circumstances. Any mommy worth her salt has to know that can't be true. Because no matter how sweet our little bundles of joy are, the day will come when we see each of them do their first thing wrong—snatch a toy, smack a playmate, deliberately steal a cookie when you said no, "accidentally" hit the newborn baby brother with a Magna Doodle.

By the way, those "accidents" with the newborn—when the next oldest child is acting so lovey-dovey and the baby somehow ends up getting hurt—our family had a name for them. When Joshua was born—the first in a string of seven Curtis kids born in ten years—Samantha was thirteen and Jasmine was seven. With a stream of visitors coming to meet the new baby, Jasmine reacted to her perceived dethroning by staging elaborate puppet shows and raffles for our guests. A little over the top, but at least a constructive way to handle those feelings of jealousy.

But Jasmine wasn't in denial about her feelings, and she actually was able to laugh at her own coping mechanisms. She was the one who came up with the term *shooganoona* to describe those times when she'd hug the baby just a little too tight, squeeze his cheek a little too hard. It was a word to describe that sibling ambivalence—"I love this baby, but I don't love how he's taking my parents away from me. I want to play with him, but I want to hurt him too."

That word—*shooganoona*—was a blessing because it put a name to something that we didn't have a name for. It made it possible to discuss the feelings and laugh about how crazy they

The Art of Apology

Let's face it, none of our kids are going to grow up to be perfect. They're going to make mistakes, break things, and hurt people—just like you and me. Here's how I taught my kids to make an authentic apology:

• Put yourself in the other's shoes—have compassion.
• Let go of guilt and pride—an apology isn't about winning or losing.
• Be sincere—no icy tone, eyeball rolls, or shoulder shrugs.
• Keep it simple—"I'm sorry."
• Avoid qualifiers like "I'm sorry you feel that way." They only add fuel to the fire, since everyone knows they mean you're not sorry at all.

can make us. It helped defuse them, so in the end there were fewer shooganoonas in the house.

Just the other day, when Tripp came back from visiting Jasmine's family and their newborn fourth, I asked how their two-year-old was handling not being the baby anymore.

"Oh, you know, a shooganoona here and there, but she's doing okay."

What I really like about the shooganoona thing is that it brought out in the open something that might have remained hidden. When feelings remain hidden they create confusion, shame, and guilt. When you bring them out and talk about them, maybe even laugh at the foolishness of them, you take away the power of the feelings to dominate your behavior.

Children need to learn, and a lot of adults need to be reminded, that feelings are not right or wrong. It's our actions that are right or wrong. Can you remember as a child being afraid of your feelings, afraid that you were a bad person just for having them? Remember to tell your children that if they have feelings that worry them to talk to you about them. And if you want your children to continue to confide in you, don't react harshly to their problems with feelings. Talk instead about making good choices where actions are concerned. And pray together.

More than anything, I want my children to be honest with themselves and with others, to take responsibility for their feelings and their actions, and to always be willing to work to do better.

Maria Montessori said, "The first idea that the child must acquire is the difference between good and evil." I agree. But in this modern age of moral relativism, it's unfashionable to be so black and white about behavior. And so a mommy might say, "I don't think Dylan likes it when you take his toy away," rather than, "Taking Dylan's toy is wrong." Hear the difference?

Language is powerful. Words are the tools that help us perceive the world in certain ways. So we need to give our children the language of good and bad, right and wrong, from the get-go.

We also need to lovingly confront them when they do something wrong, because while a toddler sneaking a cookie may not seem like a big deal, a teen shoplifting a CD is.

In dealing with my own children's wrongdoing, one incident stands out as a defining moment. Back in my homeschooling days, I used some reading comprehension workbooks with my kids in which they read one page of text and on the next answered questions about what they'd read. With four kids in different levels of the series, I depended on the teacher's guide for answers when checking their work; otherwise I'd have been up all night.

One afternoon while the kids were out playing, I was checking Matt's second-grade fill-in-the-blanks assignment. All was automatic pilot till I came to the blank on which he'd written "Answers will vary."

Yes, that was the answer in the teacher's manual to let me know that this open-ended question could have a variety of different answers from different children. And so Matt was caught cheating. He'd copied all his answers from the teacher's manual.

I didn't know whether to laugh or to cry. It hardly seemed worth it for him to have cheated on such simple work, and it sure seemed silly that he had mindlessly copied the phrase that would give him away. And yet it was a serious matter, because I needed to confront Matt about his sin.

The important thing was that I found out the first time it happened. I knew that for sure because there were other instances of "answers will vary" in previous lessons. Because he got caught the first time—and was immediately confronted (see the next section about contrition for how)—I could hope it would be his last. How much harder would it have been if he'd gotten away with it? He might have continued seizing opportunities to cheat, each time making it a little more difficult to give up his secret sin.

The other thing I learned was to trust God that he would somehow get me involved when my kids did something wrong. Time and time again God has been gracious to let me know immediately when my kids have strayed. Something always happens so I find out when my kids do something wrong. I've told them it's a sign of how much God loves them, that he just doesn't want them straying even for the briefest time.

Building integrity in my kids means keeping them honest about who they are in the Lord and what is going on in their lives. It means each member of the family needs to be honest with himself and everyone else in the family, as Jasmine was about her penchant for shooganoonas. It means loving confrontation when one is caught in sin and help in overcoming it.

The thing is, because God gave us free will, the potential for good and evil lies within each of us. My own experience is that when I gave my life to Christ, I didn't stop sinning completely (though a lot of things cleared up right away!), but I did begin to see my sin clearly and could be truthful about it. Sin no longer had any power over me.

That's what I want for my children. I know they will not always be perfect, but by building their integrity I will be equipping them to deal with the reality of sin—by being 110 percent honest and by trusting God to help them do a little better—one day at a time.

Contrition: Five Steps to Freedom

What happens when wrongdoing becomes a habit? What happens when despite your best efforts, your child continues to lie, for instance?

It can take you by surprise, especially if you've had a couple kids you had to correct about something only once or twice to get them back on track. What happens when one continues to break your trust, so you begin to question everything he says? Did he really make his bed? Feed the cat? Have permission to borrow that plastic rocket from his friend next door?

Maybe it's because with more kids I've had more confrontations with ongoing problems than less-encumbered moms, but I've been extra motivated to nip negative behavior patterns in the bud. Whether it's a major problem like lying or stealing or an annoying habit like whining or nail biting, I know I need to equip my child with whatever it takes to get over it before one of the younger kids decides to try it out herself!

That's how I came up with my Five Steps to Freedom.

Put together through many sessions in the laundry room (where I've always done my best thinking), my plan began with an appreciation for the wonderful gift God has given us in our ability to change.

Kids aren't the only ones with sin in their lives, after all. What do we grown-ups do when we find God spotlighting some area of our lives he'd like to see more conformed to his image? Most of us don't find it easy to deal with correction. But since becoming a believer, I've discovered that a follower of Christ never needs to fear, resist, or feel helpless when confronted with character flaws. Because we know through God's grace, we never have to stay the same. I become better when I'm willing to do two simple yet profound things: admit my need, and ask God's help.

I was well into adulthood when I learned how simple this is. I didn't want my children to have to wait that long. How could I equip them to accept correction without fear or defensiveness? Was there a way to help them embrace the need for change in their lives? How could I make it easier for them to become all that God intended them to be?

In the face of bad habits, I wanted to do more than change their behavior; I wanted to affect my children's hearts. I wanted them to develop the confidence to meet their problems head-on and to find the joy in change.

If this sounds like something you want to try with your children, there are two basic requirements:

1. **Become a model.** Use the steps yourself, embracing the need for change in your own life.
2. **Be willing to take the time to walk your children through the steps needed for change**—carefully and lovingly for success.

Many of the corrections we give our children are on-the-spot reproof. Most of the time we find ourselves dealing with problems as they occur, when our emotions and their defenses are high. Though this type of correction is necessary, its success is limited, usually of short duration. It doesn't equip the child to make a permanent change. When you find yourself correcting the same child for the same thing over and over, you will know it's time to release yourself and your child from the bondage of a negative behavior pattern. It's time to try what I've found works.

When you've identified an ongoing problem (whining, carelessness, or destructive behavior), spend some time preparing for a special talk with your child. Ask God for wisdom, guidance, and strength. Ask him, through you, to touch the heart of the child he loves. At some time when things are going well, and your child is not in trouble, arrange for some quiet time to sit down together.

1. Describe the Problem

"Tommy, we need to talk about something really important. You've lied to me several times in the past two weeks. Lies are like weeds in the garden: if we don't get rid of them, they spread and take over. [Children need illustrations rather than abstractions.] The more you lie, the harder it will be to stop. I love you, and I want to help you before the lying gets bigger. I know with God's help you can learn to tell the truth all the time."

2. Discuss the Moral Basis

"It's a sin to lie. Remember the commandment: 'Thou shalt not bear false witness.' God wants us to tell the truth. And remember Jesus told us he is the Way, the Truth, and the Life. Think how important the truth is if Jesus himself is the Truth." (Of course, things like nail biting and whining are not sins but bad habits, so just talk about them in terms of self-improvement, being the best we can be.)

This is a good place to bring out the Bible to show your child specific references. Even if your child is not yet reading, this will leave an impression of our reliance on God's Word for wisdom in handling our everyday problems.

3. Outline the Consequences

"Since lying is a sin, it separates you from God. God wants to keep you near to him. He wants you to tell the truth, no matter how hard it is. And your daddy and I—though we love you so much—will not be able to trust you. We've already felt how uncomfortable that is. When you always tell the truth, you let people know they can count on you."

Here you can offer illustrations from familiar stories with relevant themes—in this instance, "The Boy Who Cried Wolf." This is also the time to set up potential punishments or rewards: for example, nail polish for a nail biter who calls it quits, making restitution for damaged property, writing lines for disrespect.

4. Ask for a Commitment to Change

"I have confidence in you. And I know if you ask for God's help, he'll help you give up this bad habit. He'll give you the strength to always tell the truth. If you want to change, the first step is to make a decision. Are you willing to stop lying?"

5. End with Encouragement and Prayer

"When I was young someone once told me that with God all things are possible. I know that's true because he's helped me with many changes I've needed to make in my own life. I remember when I had a problem with being mean to my sister.

146

I asked God to help me change, and he did. If you ask God to help you, I know he will. Let's pray together and ask him to help you always tell the truth."

Here I've scripted a one-dimensional example of what you might say to your child, but let him talk to you too. If you're discussing your child's nail biting and realize that it's being caused by anxiety because of a new baby in the house, be sensitive to the fact that you may need to do some work yourself to help your child feel more secure. Sometimes bad habits or behavior are symptoms of deeper problems. Only through careful listening will you learn if there is more to the behavior than meets the eye. Ask God for guidance.

Your Part Begins Now

Once you've taken your child through the five steps, there are two more you must do on your own. The first is continued prayer. The second is close observation of your child's behavior. You need to know when your child has shown the smallest progress, so you can encourage him mightily.

Like the problem I shared earlier about Sophia's whining. After going through the Five Steps with her, though she didn't stop altogether immediately, I stayed on the lookout to detect the smallest change in tone. When I saw even the slightest change, I'd hug her and say, "Thank you for not whining." Then her voice would come down a few more notches.

Like adults, children sometimes change not in a flash but in small increments.

The Five Steps can be used from the age of three or four. Before that, the child does not have the cognitive ability to understand; that's why reasoning with a younger child is ineffective.

I've called this approach "Five Steps to Freedom" for a reason. Negative behavior and bad habits hold us in bondage. Each opportunity you have to lovingly walk your child through these steps takes you beyond the here-and-now problem. By teaching your child to face his problems squarely and take responsibility, by reminding him that we don't have to change by ourselves, that we serve a God who wants to help us become better each day, you will be building his character.

As you build his dependence on God, you are truly setting him free.

Generosity: Entertaining Angels

"Mine!"

"I wan' it!"

"Gimme dat!"

From the moment we hear our children give expression to their human self-centeredness, our job will be to help them learn to get past it. While people often mangle the Bible verse, saying "money is the root of all evil"—the Bible really says "the love of money is the root of all kinds of evil"—one could safely say that self-centeredness is the root of all evil.

It's not easy. But if we want our children to experience lives well lived, we must do everything we can to teach and model and in all ways possible share what it means to give sacrificially. The Bible is emphatic about it:

Good will come to him who is generous.

Psalm 112:5

The righteous give without sparing.

Proverbs 21:26

A generous man will himself be blessed,
    for he shares his food with the poor.

Proverbs 22:9

The Lord Jesus himself said: "It is more blessed to give than to receive."

Acts 20:35

Now, I'm not one to use the Bible to clobber people. It's just that I grew up without it and only came to know anything about what was in it in my later years. Since I've lived only a third of my life with its help, I really appreciate how God knows what's best for us.

It's good for us to learn to be free of our selfishness. And good for the many people all over the world, as well as right here in our backyard, who need help from those who've been blessed with more.

Listen to what Paul wrote Timothy: "Command those who are rich in this present world not to be arrogant nor to put their hope in wealth, which is so uncertain, but to put their hope in God, who richly provides us with everything for our enjoyment. Command them to do good, to be rich in good deeds, and to be generous and willing to share" (1 Tim. 6:17–18).

Especially if you're struggling paycheck to paycheck, you may not think of yourself as rich. But you probably have a place to live, a car, food in the refrigerator, and education for your children. Compared to the poor of other countries, even the poorest Americans have an abundance.

It's all a matter of perspective.

While in high school, my daughter Jasmine went on a short-term mission trip to Mexico. Coming home, she stood inside our door and looked around in wonder. She told us all of a family who lived in a one-room, dirt-floor house the size of our foyer—a family with five or six kids, one who seemed to have cerebral palsy.

"But they had so much joy," she said. "And they wanted to share everything they could."

So they asked the American teens to come to dinner, killing two chickens in honor of the occasion.

I don't think Jasmine was ever the same.

Wanting to make generosity easy and exciting for my kids, I looked for ways that would be tangible and meaningful on a child's level. Remember, children are not abstract but concrete. Giving money or watching their parents write checks is less satisfying than doing something real, like going to the grocery store and buying a cartful of groceries for a family that's struggling while Daddy looks for more work.

When I make trips to donate used clothing and other items, I take my kids with me. Madeleine was actually very surprised the first time she went to the Goodwill store with me. "Where's the well?" she asked. It turned out that all the times I mentioned taking things to the Goodwill, she had pictured me throwing them down "the Good Well"—like the one she'd seen at Snow White's Castle in Disneyland.

At Christmas, with the cultural me-me mentality, I'm grateful for anything that will get my kids focused on others. One church we attended for a number of years participated in Prison Fellowship's Angel Tree project, where each family plucked the name and gift list of a child of an imprisoned parent from a tree, then bought and wrapped presents for volunteers to hand-deliver.

If you like that idea but your church doesn't do it, look in local banks and stores at Christmastime for similar trees with names of local needy children. Shopping and wrapping for real children means more than watching Mom and Dad give money.

One Christmas ministry any family anywhere can participate in is Operation Christmas Child, a ministry of Samaritan's Purse (www.samaritanspurse.org). It's really become my favorite because it's so easily grasped by kids. What you do is wrap or decorate a shoe box and then fill it with small toys, school supplies, hygiene items, candy, even small pieces of clothing. You'd be surprised how much wonderful stuff you can fit in a shoe box! And there's something very immediate and special when a child shops, then fills the box knowing another child in a faraway country will open it and be surprised and delighted by the things he picked out.

The boxes are classified by gender and age categories, so you can have each of your children fill a box for someone just like them—even include a note and a picture. It's real, personal, and gives a child the opportunity to truly feel the blessing of being able to give.

Another child-appealing way to give is with World Vision's gift catalog, which features gifts in every price range from a $15 pair of rabbits to a $12,500 well. The catalog is full of pictures of children and families enjoying the gifts. For instance, under a picture of a girl holding a baby goat, the copy reads:

> The early morning bleating of a dairy goat is a happy sound for children. They know it's ready to be milked! A goat provides a family with fresh milk, cheese and added income when they sell offspring, and any extra food at the market. Our best-value, best-selling gift, every year!

We were so excited to find this catalog that we agreed to receive only one smallish Christmas gift that year and to use the money we would have spent on more stuff to help build a home for a family in Africa. Since then, some members of the family have asked for birthday gifts from the catalog—to be sent to people who are more in need than we will ever be.

And another year-round way to personalize generosity is through World Vision's child sponsorship, which has become even more up close and personal as you can pick your sponsored child online—by gender, age, country, even by birthday. For twenty-six dollars a month you can make a difference in a child's life. Some families—like my daughter Samantha's—sponsor one child for each of their birth children, keeping their pictures out as though they are members of the family and reading together all the correspondence they receive.

We adults may have our tithing down. But that kind of giving can't be passed on. It is in these concrete acts of giving that we can build a foundation of generosity for our children.

And don't forget that generosity is not just about material things. It's about giving of our time, our energy, ourselves. The lessons in these aspects of generosity are ongoing as opportunities arise in everyday living.

Is it easy to let go of self-centeredness? No. But as our children grow, the more they come to understand the greatness of the gift we received through Jesus, the easier it will be for them to think less of themselves and more of others.

Part 3

Pleasures

Whatever is true, whatever is noble, whatever is right, whatever is pure, whatever is lovely, whatever is admirable—if anything is excellent or praiseworthy—think about such things.

Philippians 4:8

5

The Keys to Cultural Heritage

Delighting in your family—having good times, building memories—is what this part of *The Mommy Manual* is all about. And if it seems strange to dedicate equal space to work and play, just remember: having fun is serious business.

At least for parents who want their children to have the best. Your little one's idea of fun today may be kicking off his socks, pursuing the cat's tail, or endlessly dropping his spoon from his high chair in a game of "Pick It Up, Mommy!" But sooner than you can imagine, he'll be asking, "Can I go with the guys to see *The Never-Ending Night of the Living Dead Alien Werewolves?*"

What will you say then?

That's the thing about parenthood—it's headed somewhere. While some might prefer living moment by moment, you just can't live moment by moment and end up with kids who respect the choices you make for them and who are able to make good choices themselves.

Even in the area of having fun, parents need a vision for the future, a strong sense of purpose, and commitment to do whatever it takes to stay on course with the vision and the purpose.

Fifty years ago, things were different. With the culture wrapped securely in the Judeo-Christian ethic, parents could send their kids off to the Saturday matinee—admission just twenty-five cents!—and trust that their innocence wouldn't be shattered. Cynics may turn up their noses at yesteryear's wholesome fare—TV's *My Three Sons, Leave It to Beaver, The Brady Bunch, The Partridge Family,* and *The Cosby Show*—but, let's face it, the world in those days was safer for kids. And parents didn't have to work so hard.

Today, our culture is chockful of entertainment opportunities: places to go, books to read, music to hear, movies to see. In the summer alone, more than a hundred movies are released. When your kids are old enough to pay attention, they'll be pestering you to see this one and that. Their friends will bring over music and video games to play, some of which you might not like.

The truth is that a lot of the entertainment available to kids today is of a type that's prone to enslave them. Spend a little time watching MTV to get a clear idea of the kind of propaganda your kids are getting concerning fashion and sexual conduct. Then block it from your channel list for the rest of your children's lives.

No flying-by-the-seat-of-your-pants parenting will work today—not when a movie that would have been R-rated ten years ago is now PG-13, and not when so many other parents are MIA, allowing their kids to see *Dumb and Dumber* or *American Pie.* You know, there are some R-rated movies I wouldn't mind sitting next to Jesus to see (*The Mission* comes to mind). But there is some supposedly "lighter fare" out there I would be ashamed of—full of crude, lewd, and rude behavior.

The only protective layer between your kids and a lot of mindless entertainment pushed at them is you. As a parent today you need not only to develop a clear vision of what values you hold dear but also to communicate the vision to your kids in a winsome way.

Just as you start in the early years to build a work ethic, consider building a play ethic. You'll begin building early, when you set the stage by reading to your child, and in later years watching movies together, eventually discussing themes and teaching her how to choose the best herself.

Bringing up a discerning child is not just a matter of setting taboos; it's more about searching out worthwhile stuff. Because even though the Scholastic Book catalogs—sent home from school so you can buy books for your kids—are loaded with dark and negative content, they still contain a lot of tried and true. Because in today's culture entertainment runs the gamut from the bloody brutality of *Kill Bill 2* to the whimsical warmth of *Finding Nemo*. There really is a lot of uplifting, sensitive, good, and noble material to choose from.

Beyond choosing wisely for your kids, you have the opportunity to enable your children to choose wisely for themselves. In the sixteen or so years you have available to develop your children's personal discernment, the essence of what you want to teach them is this: when it comes to making wise entertainment choices, it's not so much about turning away from the bad as it is turning toward the good.

Turning toward the good does require something more than parental training, though. It requires a believing heart and the guidance of the Holy Spirit.

I know because I spent many years myself without that kind of faith and guidance.

Many things changed when my husband and I became believers. It was as though we'd been living in a dark, cluttered basement—though never seeing it as so—that was suddenly illuminated for what it was. And then as if someone took our hands to lead us up into the real world of light and wonder.

That was what it felt like when I put my trust and faith in Jesus.

We had five children then, and as I taught them Bible stories, I was learning them too. I had no idea the Bible had so many wise things to say.

But it was more than learning about the Bible. It was also learning about me. As time went by, occasionally I'd remember choices I'd made for myself and my children that now seemed so blatantly wrong. I was startled to remember I'd taken my oldest daughter, Samantha, to see *Alien* when she was ten years old.

What in the world was I thinking?

Obviously, I wasn't thinking at all. I was a parent without a clue, a parent without a plan, a parent without the Holy Spirit to guide me in choosing wisely for my child.

I see parents like that often at the video store. Just last week I overheard this conversation between a dad and seven- or eight-year-old daughter studying the rack of horror movies:

"Dad, can we get *Friday the 13th*?"

"We already saw that one, remember? How about *Freddy vs. Jason*?"

It's hard for me to fathom how a child can process that kind of material. When I was eleven or so I saw *The Blob*, a 1950s sci-fi film about a gelatinous, well, blob, which oozed under doors and consumed anything it touched. Think "fifties production values" and imagine how laughably campy the film would look today. Yet for months I was terrified that the Blob would come oozing under my bedroom door and there would be no more Barbara. I mean it, I was terrified.

Remember how I wrote in the beginning of the book about seeing the world through children's eyes? Even when it comes to entertainment, we can't just take anything about our kids for granted.

Let's start from the beginning. As you hold your newborn in your arms, you are everything—your baby's One Stop Shop for food, warmth, protection, and—ta da!—entertainment. You giggle and coo and make funny faces and talk in a high-pitched voice, all the things science has gone to great lengths to prove are universal baby attention-holders.

This is the beginning of a bonding process that continues as you cradle your little one in your lap and read stories, as you listen to music and watch movies together. Through trips to the zoo, amusement parks, museums. You are the person your child trusts and in whose footsteps she wants to follow.

Everything you do with your child in the early years will have a special impact. If, for example, your child's first trip to an art museum is with you rather than with her fourth-grade class years down the road, she will always have a special feeling about art. If your child hears a wide variety of music at home, including classical, she will be more interested in music later on.

Also, God may have planted a special gift in your child—artistic ability, musical talent, a flair for drama—that will be more likely to find release with early exposure to the arts. Why wait until she's in school for it to be revealed? Don't you want to be the one who first sees it?

From an early age, my son Benjamin was fascinated with opera. When he was eight years old, I got tickets for the two of us to see *The Magic Flute*. He sat mesmerized through the whole three-and-a-half-hour production. At intermission and afterward, strangers came up to me and commented on his concentration.

Now, you need to understand that Ben is a really masculine guy. He played Pop Warner football and swam on the swim team. As a teenager, he organized Air Soft wars, where he and his buddies wore camouflage and protective gear and strategized and stalked each other in the woods around our house. (Note to moms: let your boys be boys!) Most recently, he's loved playing rugby, boasting of his bruises and almost dislocating his shoulder a time or two.

But through it all, Ben has loved music and singing. He pursued voice lessons and starred in high school musicals, including Curly in *Oklahoma*. Last year he entered college as a voice major, though he's working on starting a rugby team there too.

Ask me now, ten years after that opera performance, if I'm glad I got those tickets to *The Magic Flute*. I couldn't be more delighted, having shared in the earliest part of Ben's musical journey.

No matter what kind of background you come from, even a disadvantaged one like mine, you can give so much more to your children. And whether you're just discovering for the first time or rediscovering anew what an exciting world we live in, these years with your young children can be rich and rewarding in terms of sharing our cultural heritage while building closer bonds.

So, in this section of *The Mommy Manual*, I want to show you first how to:

- build a special bond with your child through early reading
- choose and get the most out of books and movies
- introduce your child to the arts

This intimate approach is one that enables you to give your child the keys to our cultural heritage. Then if there is something she is more curious about and wants to pursue, you will be part of it. In addition, she will be looking to you as a trusted guide to entertainment later on.

Reading 0–2 Years: Books Are Best

Even if you never really connected with reading before, you may discover as a parent, through reading daily with your own little one, that it's a lot of fun. One of the greatest benefits of having kids is the opportunity it gives us to grow and to change. The first step to putting your child on the path to a lifelong love of reading is to fall in love with reading yourself.

And falling in love with reading isn't that hard to do. Take it from someone who's been reading to kids for thirty-five years: children's books are fun to read, especially when you know what to look for.

Looking for the right books is important. There's a lot out there to choose from. And there's a lot to avoid. If you're going to take the time to cuddle up and read a book to your child, why not make it the best, especially if your time is limited?

What makes some books better than others? Here's what C. S. Lewis, author of *The Lion, the Witch and the Wardrobe* and six other books in the beloved Narnia series, had to say: "I never wrote down to anyone. . . . It certainly is my opinion that a book worth reading only in childhood is not worth reading even then" ("Sometimes Fairy Stories May Say Best What's to Be Said," *On Stories: And Other Essays on Literature* by C. S. Lewis).

To start with, the best children's literature, like all literature, presents some problem that needs resolution, as in *Caps for Sale*, in which the cap seller must get his caps back from the rascally monkeys. In the end the story shows how the problem is resolved and reestablishes feelings of security and well-being, as in *Good Dog, Carl*. Better yet, it will teach a lesson, very subtly, along the way, as in *Where's Our Mama?*, which reminds children to stay in the same place when they are lost while validating each listener's belief that her mama is the best.

Don't Tell Me, Show Me

Many entertaining and engaging stories carry an extra bonus: a theme that reinforces a value or virtue. The message in *The Rainbow Fish* may be clear to adults: pride isolates a person, and sharing feels good. Even though the theme is never stated directly, we can easily put it into words ourselves. The young mind works differently. A statement of theme would mean nothing to a child. But through the story of the rainbow fish's conflict and resolution, the theme can have a powerful impact on the character of a child.

Children, especially, think and perceive on a concrete level. During the preschool years they are incapable of abstract thinking. Teaching them about kindness, generosity, and courage can take place only through stories.

Most of us—children and adults—would rather have someone show us why something works than tell us. Very few enjoy being clobbered with ideas. We'd rather hear stories. Experts refer to the themes underlying plot lines as subliminal messages. These messages make stories powerful teaching devices.

Finding and Choosing Books

If you can afford it, try to assemble a home library for your children. When your kids see you buying books, they realize that books have value and worth. There are so many inexpensive paperback editions out—with the same wonderful illustrations as the expensive hardcover—that for the cost of a video rental you can get a book or two to have around for many years.

Books are a worthy investment. Children treat books like old friends; they want to spend a lot of time with the ones they really enjoy. No children's book is ever read just once. Children return again and again to a favorite book rather than losing interest or outgrowing it. They pore over the pictures, discovering new details, thinking to themselves, and talking to each other about them.

Trust me, a good book will hold your child's attention much longer than most toys—and books have the advantage of not missing pieces or cluttering up your house as much. Books also have a longer lifespan than most toys. Books have a way of growing up with a child. I've heard of college-bound teens who've asked their parents not to get rid of their childhood libraries because they want them for their own children.

Just how nostalgic can grown-ups get for their old favorites? Ask the buyers of *Jellybeans for Breakfast*, a book popular with little girls growing up in the early seventies, which now sells for more than $150 on eBay and Amazon to young moms who want to read their favorites to their own children.

As for used books, check secondhand stores, flea markets, and garage sales. But do make sure they're in good shape before buying them. If you want your child to respect books, they must be in good condition.

Let grandparents, friends, and family know that you would love to receive books for baby gifts. If you have several children and they receive books for gifts, you will build a respectable library faster than you think.

Public libraries are a good resource for borrowing books (they also have sales of old books sometimes), and trips to the

Guidelines for Buying Books

With an unlimited budget for books, you could build a library of everything out there for kids. Thank goodness our budgets are limited. That way we are forced to look for the best!

Is this book attractive to children?

Is this book fun to read—over and over again?

Does this book have staying power—a timeless theme or classic message?

Does this book reinforce (or at least challenge) the values I want for my family?

Does this book invite parent-child interaction?

library have a lot of charm. But here you would be wise to give your child a lot of guidance. Many books have themes incompatible with the needs of children and perhaps with your own convictions. I always page through books my children pick before actually checking them out. I have weeded out some real junk that way.

If your library has a story hour, check to see which book the librarian is reading before taking your child. Stories about witches, goblins, and ghosts, for instance (standard fare during Halloween season) are never appropriate for toddlers, who are not yet capable of distinguishing between reality and fantasy.

But those are issues you will face later on. Books for babies are straightforward and innocent, picturing familiar things or telling things simply like *Goodnight Moon*, which has a rhythm and poetry that sounds irresistible.

Cuddle Up

From the time you can hold your baby in a sitting position, you can share the joy of reading together. Reading before bedtime is a wonderful tradition to begin early on, but try not to limit reading to only one time of day—try after lunch or after playtime too. In addition to spending quality time together, you will be planting some pre-reading skills that will help him later on. Early read-alouds build good listening habits, laying the foundation for a child who can cooperate and concentrate, who will develop good comprehension skills.

So do start early!

While holding your baby in your lap, look at the book in front of you together at a comfortable level. Exaggerate the care with which you pick up just the corner of the page and turn it. If the text seems too complicated, use your own words—but remember, the child's ability to understand is always well beyond the words he can say. Your voice and inflection play an important part in his understanding. As you read the text, point, sliding your finger smoothly just under the words.

This simple practice of reading with your little ones has long-term benefits far beyond simply building a love of reading. It reinforces an intimate bond, a trust in you as the one who knows and understands your child best, who can be counted on for choosing amusement. As he grows, your child will be more inclined to listen to and trust your voice when it comes to entertainment choices.

Getting Ready

Who knew something so simple could be so varied, because you can read three ways:

1. comprehensively—spending time on each page to discuss and ask questions
2. technically—noting sentences, words, letters ("Do you see an *S* on this page?")
3. dramatically—presenting material uninterruptedly, with focus only on story, holding any questions or comments till the end

Rhythm and Repetition

Two characteristics often found in children's books are rhythm and repetition. Both work to keep the child focused on the book. Skillful children's authors know this will keep a child coming back again and again. As you read, emphasize the rhythm and repetition in the text. Besides making a book more fun for you and your child, each also makes it easy for the child to memorize the text and "read" it on his own.

It's a good idea to do some of each, though the first and third are where you'll spend the most time. Above all, have a good time! Reading with your child can be so freeing, especially if you've always wanted to be a little less reserved! Now's the time to be dramatic, and remember that any parent can be Oscar-worthy in the eyes of an admiring child. Make stories come alive through variations in tempo, pitch, or inflection. Create character voices, make background noises, use hands and arms to illustrate emotions.

Since you will be reading stories more than once, you might as well make them fun. (And how! I once figured out I'd read *Go, Dog, Go* at least six hundred times!)

Reading Recommendations

After thirty-five years of reading books to my own children as well as to students, I have a good idea which deserve more than a casual read or two, which can please now and later, and which can even stand up to a few hundred readings (don't laugh until you've had a few children!).

With twelve kids and two parents who love books, our family has built quite a children's library, which lines the bottom shelves in my office. Along with a cozy couch, they invite my children to read while Mama writes.

All this by way of saying I didn't have to go very far to find these books I'm about to share with you. I've simply pulled out the best from my own children's shelves.

The fact that some were pretty worn—having spent a lot of time in children's laps and hands—made them easier to sight on the shelves. I left behind their wallflower cousins and chose the ones whose dance cards were always full.

In my recommendations, I have listed the date of first publication so you will get a sense of the timelessness of stories with true kid appeal. However, I have checked carefully to make sure of availability. Out-of-print books are usually available on Amazon.

These books have been a major part of my life for many years. So it is with great pleasure that I introduce these faithful family friends. As you get to know them, I am sure you will love them too.

While these books can captivate the attention of very young children, their appeal and value extend well beyond the early years. A four- or five-year-old will find much of interest in Richard Scarry's *Best Word Book Ever*, for example. Other books, such as *Caps for Sale* or *Noisy Nora*, will later double as your child's first readers.

READ-ALOUD STORIES

Best Word Book Ever by Richard Scarry, Golden Press, 1963. Every one of my children, from the oldest (now thirty-five) to the current toddler, has found plenty to hold their attention for hours in this terrific vocabulary builder brimming over with pictures of almost everything a child could possibly learn to name.

Brown Bear, Brown Bear, What Do You See? by Bill Martin Jr., illustrated by Eric Carle, Holt and Company, 1967. A story built on rhythm and repetition, highlighting colors and animals. Little ones love this first memory stretcher.

Caps for Sale by Esphyr Slobodkina, Scholastic, 1940. Be dramatic! Shake your fists! Stomp your feet! You and your toddler will have so much fun with this wonderful story, in which common sense prevails over temper tantrums.

Chicken Soup with Rice by Maurice Sendak, Scholastic, 1962. Another R & R (rhythm and repetition), this one filled with a feeling of humor and impossible to read without a smile.

Good Dog, Carl by Alexandra Day, Simon & Schuster, 1985. A wonderful introduction to story sequence—plot, scenes, characters, emotion. (Will they get the house in order before Mother comes home?) And all this without a single word of text! Toddlers and parents can have a lot of fun with this engagingly illustrated tale.

Goodnight Moon by Margaret Wise Brown, Harper & Row, 1947. If you could do a survey of children's favorite books and ask children themselves, this gem of a book would surely top the list. A bunny gets ready for sleep, saying good night to each special object he sees from his bed. A soft and soothing farewell at the end of any little one's busy day.

Jamberry by Bruce Degen, Harperfestival, 1985. An energetic romp through the colorful world of berries with a rollicking rhyme-spouting bear and a straw-hatted boy. There's so much to celebrate!

"More More More" Said the Baby by Vera B. Williams, William Morrow & Co., 1990. A trio of love stories—three toddlers enjoying tender moments with father, grandmother, and mother. Catchy toddler words, bright vivid pictures. Natural, wholesome, current, very appealing.

Noisy Nora by Rosemary Wells, Scholastic, 1973. Poor Nora! The loveable mousette experiences all the pangs of the child-in-the-middle, caught between the demands of Baby Brother and bossiness of Big Sister. Catchy meter and playful illustrations make for a wonderfully satisfying mouse's tale.

On Mother's Lap by Ann Herbert Scott, Scholastic, 1992. An Eskimo boy finds a lot of room on Mother's lap for all his favorite things but thinks there's none for his baby sister. Mother shows him there's room for all. A wonderful remedy for new-baby blues.

Read-Aloud Bible Stories, Volumes 1–4, by Ella K. Lindvall, Moody, 1982–95. These large volumes with bold, full-page illustrations on one side and simple text on the other have a lot of kid appeal. One unusual feature is that Jesus's face is never seen, thus avoiding some of the stereotypes and allowing room for children's imagination. Bible stories retold with rhythm, repetition, and loads of enthusiasm. For example, when the apostles fish where Jesus tells them: "Big fish/ little fish/ wiggly fish/ Oh my!"

The Runaway Bunny by Margaret Wise Brown, Harper & Row, 1942. Another must-have from the author of *Goodnight Moon*, the story of Everybunny, who like every typical toddler wants to assert his independence from Mother while being reminded she will always be there for him. Beautifully illustrated, a message with lasting value.

Shoes by Elizabeth Winthrop, Harper & Row, 1986. A rollicking, rhyming tribute to a toddler's most-loved item of apparel. Just for fun!

The Very Hungry Caterpillar (also *The Very Busy Spider* and *The Grouchy Ladybug*) by Eric Carle, Philomel Books, 1984. A children's library with no books by Eric Carle would be like a chocolate chip cookie with no chips. This author understands how to captivate even the most easily distracted child. Read this one with lots of finger drama and chomping noises, and your child is sure to be delighted.

Where's Our Mama? by Diane Goode, Scholastic, 1991. Such a sweet story! Two children who have lost their mama have trouble finding her only because they see her as the best, the wisest, the most beautiful. The gendarme (French policeman) is astonished to finally find that she is just a mama like everyone else's. For fun, read it with your best French accent!

BOARD BOOKS

Many toddler favorites have been released as board books. Collect a few favorites to keep in a basket for your child to "read" independently until old enough to take proper care of the ones with paper pages you read aloud. Also recommended, exclusively in board book format:

All Aboard Noah's Ark (also *In the Beginning, Baby Moses, Jonah and the Whale, Little David and the Giant*) by Mary Josephs, Random House, 1994. Small, pudgy books that fit well in small, pudgy hands, with little flaps to peek under on every page. Each tells a familiar story in simple, childish language.

Little Duck's Friends (also others in the series of Squeeze-and-Squeak Books) by Muff Singer, Joshua Morris, 1994. Special pages cut around a soft plastic duck invite the child to press and make him squeak. The storyline explains, in rhyme, how each animal has special gifts. So does Baby!

Pat the Bunny by Dorothy Kunhardt, Golden Press, 1940. Lots of people give this one as a shower gift. An unabashedly old-fashioned and delightful book with lots of "fingers on" fun for tots. A must for all.

Reading 2–5 Years: A Reading-Rich Environment

Some day down your child's road, books will become instruments of learning. But for now, they're for fun (although there are often lessons as a subtle subtext). The more you reinforce that fun, the less inclined your child will be to think of reading as a drag later on.

So make reading as pleasurable and attractive as possible.

I mentioned earlier the importance of your child seeing you read. In addition to reading to him, find times to read side-by-side—you engrossed in your book while he "reads" his. Make it a habit to take children's books with you everywhere: to the doctor's office, the beach, Grandma's house, the bus, short trips, or vacation. Read in the morning, before naps, after dinner, before bed. Be careful never to make it seem like a chore but instead a refreshing break, something you look forward to whole-heartedly.

Have a few snuggly places to read. Make your child's solo reading extra special by creating a reading nook. This doesn't require much space. After all, a child isn't very big! Even a cozy chair or maybe just a large, comfy pillow on the floor next to a sunny window will do. Decorate with some small pictures hung at her level. I like pictures of people reading. Provide an inexpensive bookcase to hold her own books.

Begin early to teach your child how to handle books with respect. (If you grew up in a home where books were used for coasters, you might want to rethink this now that you're paying for them yourself!) When you read with your child, exaggerate the care with which you turn the pages. Teach your child when she is finished reading a book to place it upright on the shelf with the binding facing out.

Reading Recommendations

Bedtime for Frances (also *A Baby Sister for Frances*, *A Birthday for Frances*, and more) by Russell Hoban, HarperCollins, 1976. You'll surely fall in love with Frances, the little badger

Getting the Most out of Your Reading

Start a book by reading the title and the author with your child. This lets him know that a book is someone's creation. You might want to talk about the cover art and mention the name of the artist. This lets him know that a book is a collaborative effort.

Start early to help your child make the distinction between reality and fantasy. There are three kinds of books: (1) stories that really happened, as in history and biography books; (2) stories that could happen, as in *Ira Sleeps Over* (a dilemma any child could face); and (3) stories that could never happen at all (*Where the Wild Things Are*, for instance). Be sure to let your child know which kind you're reading.

Some people question using fantasy at all with children. Montessori did and said she felt toddlers couldn't distinguish between fantasy and reality because they couldn't yet think abstractly. Reality is so full of marvelous things, she reasoned, that we could easily fill the early years just teaching them all the wonders of the world, saving fantasy for later.

Likewise, some parents for religious reasons wish to avoid fantasy or even stories that have animals as characters.

I see value in fantasy, although it requires an extra amount of discernment on the part of parents to make sure that the author's message (because every author has one) is compatible with what they want their children to learn. Books with animal characters (I especially think of Russell Hoban's Frances books) can teach important lessons in charming and nonthreatening ways. Books like *Where the Wild Things Are* deal with very real and inexpressible childhood feelings, showing them resolved with security restored at the end. Remember, at this age a child cannot think abstractly. Therefore, the only way you can teach him about courage, loyalty, faith, and love is through stories.

Christian parents can get more out of books that are not specifically Christian through discussion in which they apply Christian themes. That way they are also teaching their children that their spirituality does not exist in a vacuum—it's not tied to specific times and books. It's a filter through which to view any information.

who brings the problems of childhood to life in such a warm and whimsical way. Frances's mother and father are always there to help her through her latest crisis—with serenity and a sense of humor.

The Bible Illustrated for Little Children by Ella K. Lindvall, Moody Press, 1985. Walk through the Bible with your child—from creation to Paul's imprisonment—with these gorgeously illustrated, captivatingly told one-page stories. Each story is followed by conversational questions.

The Carrot Seed by Ruth Krauss, Trophy Press, 1945. A little boy plants a seed, and though he receives a lot of discouragement, he does all he can to help it grow. His efforts are rewarded.

The Cat in the Hat (also *Fox in Socks* and *Green Eggs and Ham*) by Dr. Seuss, Random House, 1957. One of the best parts of being a parent is getting to revisit old favorites like these. These funny, fantastic books beg to be read over and over. Later, because they are as close as best friends, they will become confidence-builders as your child begins to read.

Corduroy by Don Freeman, Viking, 1968. A stuffed bear wants a home, but waiting in the department store has taken its toll. Still, a little girl falls in love with him. A tale about security and unconditional love.

Giant Steps for Little People by Kenneth N. Taylor, Tyndale, 1985. The Sermon on the Mount and the Ten Commandments, broken into "bite-sized morsels a very young child can grasp and grow on." Each page offers a spiritual truth, a practical application (with lots of opportunities for parent/child conversation), a prayer, and a memory verse. A treasure.

Go, Dog, Go by Philip D. Eastman, Random House, 1961. One of the silliest teaching books around, this book is jam-packed with adjectives and prepositions—important for later skills—but is still guaranteed to give your child a fun time. Another book that will double as an early reader eventually.

Ira Sleeps Over by Bernard Waber, Houghton Mifflin Co., 1973. How exciting to be invited to spend the night at a friend's house, but how scary to face the prospect of sleeping without your teddy bear! A childhood dilemma depicted with empathy and humor.

The Little Engine That Could by Watty Piper, Platt & Munck, 1930. A wonderful message for children: with a humble heart and a little determination, even the smallest can save the day. A classic for generations.

The Little Red Hen, various authors and publishers since 1942. Hooray for a good work ethic! The little red hen asks for but receives no help in her efforts to put bread on the table. Yet all who wouldn't help would like to eat. In a refreshingly old-fashioned triumph of moral consequences, they don't get to.

Madeline by Ludwig Bemelmans, Viking, 1958. A classic told in charming rhyme, this book opens the window to a different world, where little French girls go to boarding school and one has her appendix removed.

Make Way for Ducklings by Robert McCloskey, Viking, 1941. Such a family-values story! Mr. and Mrs. Mallard search for the perfect spot to raise their family, with some assistance from a friendly police officer. Told and illustrated with humor and warmth.

Millions of Cats by Wanda Gag, various publishers since 1928. An enchanting tale of a man who comes home with "hundreds of cats, thousands of cats, millions and billions and trillions of cats." Lots of rhythm, rhyme, and repetition make a strong point: humility can keep you from harm, and love can bring out beauty.

Peter's Chair by Ezra Jack Keats, Trophy Press, 1967. Peter faces life with a new sister—including having all his furniture painted pink. How will he learn to accept his new place in the family?

Play with Me by Marie Hall Ets, Viking, 1955. On my first read of this book, I found it a little too quiet, but that's the point. Children must get it, because they seem fascinated by this tale of a lonely girl who finds friends in the forest through cultivating patience and stillness. After reading, challenge your child to be still and quiet—a great lesson in self-control.

The Puppy Who Wanted a Boy by Jane Thayer, Scholastic, 1968. Petey the puppy wants a boy for Christmas, but his mother tells him he'll have to find one on his own. Of course, there's a happy ending!

The Rainbow Fish by Marcus Pfister, Scholastic, 1992. A new tale destined to become a classic: the story of a beautiful, proud, and selfish little fish who discovers life isn't much fun without sharing. A finely drawn message just right for children. The editions with glittery scales shimmer too!

Stone Soup by Ann McGovern, Scholastic, 1968. The hilarious tale of an old woman and the clever vagabond who convinces her that she can make soup from a stone, while persuading her to add a little of this and a little of that. Children love this story and then making soup afterward.

Where the Wild Things Are by Maurice Sendak, Harper and Row, 1963. The wildly imaginative tale of a boy sent to his room with no supper who finds his way through an emotional jungle filled with funny-looking monsters and then back to his own room. Reaffirms the old notion that there's just no place like home!

Reading 5–7 Years: Reading Rocks!

Books for this age are so exciting! What a wonder that simply by turning the pages of a book you can give your child an up-close-and-personal look at life on the other side of the globe or the other side of the century! Or serve up a tale meant to help her cope with her problems or build her character. Or share with her your history or your faith.

Your child is at an age now where she is ready to be introduced to an abundance of life, the broadest spectrum of races, places, cultures, and historical periods. She needs to know that even in our own country, even in our own hometown, not everyone lives the same way. Especially if your child lives in comfortable circumstances she needs to know that others live in need.

But she also needs to know that material circumstances don't say much at all about the things that truly make life worth living. As in *A Chair for My Mother*, a family can go through many ups and downs and yet find great joy in something small and simple.

Values-building starts earlier than we might think. At five years old, children are really beginning to size up the world and the adults around them. They have a lot of questions regarding right and wrong. They want answers.

At this age, the most appropriate way to teach values is through stories. In *The Little Red Lighthouse and the Great Gray Bridge*, children see arrogance projected onto a protagonist who isn't even human. This makes it safe to look at.

Try when you can to preview a book before reading it with your child, to understand the message. Take it from a writer: every writer has an agenda. When you read a book to your children you need to know if the agenda behind it is compatible with your own. This means you need to be very clear what your own is.

Whatever you do, don't leave your children empty to absorb the values of popular culture, of television and movies. Take a proactive approach. Have a plan; decide what's important to your family and then back it up by making sure the books you give your children, as much as the shows you let them watch, are compatible with your values.

If in doubt, skip it. There's too much good stuff out there to waste time on books that undermine the values you hold dear. And there's so much that will stretch you and your children in a positive direction.

Reading Recommendations

Alexander and the Terrible, Horrible, No Good, Very Bad Day by Judith Viorst, Aladdin, 1972. Everyone has a really bad day now and then. Alexander gives us a language for sharing it and accepting it. Contemporary and funny.

Blueberries for Sal by Robert McCloskey, Puffin Books, 1948. What happens when a little girl and a little bear wander away from their blueberry-picking mothers and switch who they follow? A beautifully illustrated story sets a lovely mood, then introduces just enough suspense for children.

A Chair for My Mother by Vera B. Williams, Mulberry, 1982. A remarkably beautiful story told by a young girl whose mother is a waitress. Since they lost all their furniture in a fire, they've been saving mother's tips in a jar so they can buy a big, comfortable chair for their whole family to enjoy—daughter, mother, and grandmother. Life has its ups and downs, but there's always lots of love.

Frog and Toad Are Friends (and other Frog and Toad books) by Arnold Lobel, Harpercollins, 1970. A pair of loveable best friends spend the summer watching out for and bringing out the best in each other. Doubles as an early reading primer.

George Shrinks by William Joyce, Scholastic, 1985. Nothing heavy, just a romp for the imagination when George dreams he is small and wakes up the size of a peanut. Your child will love the pictures, in which George flies for the mail in a toy airplane.

Goops and How to Be Them: A Manual of Manners for Polite Infants Inculcating Many Juvenile Virtues Both by Precept and Example, with 90 Drawings (also *More Goops and How to Be Them*) by Gelett Burgess, Dover Publications, republished 1968. "The Goops they lick their fingers, and the Goops they lick their knives; they spill their broth on tablecloth—Oh, they lead disgusting lives!" This old-fashioned compendium of poems on manners is just plain hilarious—and one of the easiest ways to teach children manners.

Harold and the Purple Crayon by Crockett Johnson, Harpercollins, 1955. An ingenious tale. Harold goes out for a walk with a purple crayon in his hand and draws himself all kinds of adventures, showing some common sense and good problem-solving skills along the way.

The Hole in the Dike, retold by Norma Green, Scholastic, 1974. As the author states at the end of the book, this tale was spun a hundred years ago by a woman who had never been to Holland. And yet it so symbolized the struggle of the Dutch that they erected a statue to the boy who saved his country from floods. A tale that underscores sacrifice and loyalty to one's country.

Least of All by Carol Purdy, Aladdin, 1987. The youngest of six children and the only girl, Raven Hannah is not big enough to help with any of the work on her family's farm. But when she teaches herself to read from the Bible she finds that as the first reader in the family, she has a unique gift to offer.

The Lion and the Mouse by A. J. Wood, illustrated by Ian Andrew, Millbrook Press, 1995. Aesop's classic fable, beloved by readers throughout the ages, of a mighty lion who spares the life of a mouse and is amply repaid for his mercy.

The Little House by Virginia Lee Burton, Scholastic, 1942. "Once upon a time there was a little house way out in the country.

She was a pretty Little House and she was strong and well built." The contrast between the Little House's peaceful existence with the beautiful seasons and her life when a big city grows around her makes for a touching tale. The deeper theme: progress has a price. Children will love the pictures, the happy ending, and the lesson learned by the Little House.

Little People in Tough Spots: Bible Answers for Young Children by V. Gilbert Beers, Thomas Nelson, 1992. This gem of a book shows children in an easy-to-understand way that the answers to life's problems are in the Bible. Pick a problem—"I'm scared," "I have too much to do," "Do I have to share?"—and you will find a vignette of a child here and now who faces the problem, then draws inspiration from a particular person in the Bible.

The Little Red Lighthouse and the Great Gray Bridge by Hildegarde H. Swift, Harcourt Brace, 1942. A little lighthouse on the Hudson River starts out with a little too much pride, suffers great humiliation when the George Washington Bridge is built, and finally gains a properly modest confidence when it finds that it is useful and has an important job to do.

Ox-Cart Man by Donald Hall, Viking Press, 1979. This lyrical journey through the seasons with a serene and productive nineteenth-century rural New England family will give your child (and you) a feeling for our country's heritage.

People by Peter Spier, Doubleday, 1980. An incredibly rich child-friendly resource of information about the diversity of people and cultures. Beautiful and absorbing illustrations, beginning with Adam and Eve in the Garden of Eden, then covering all sorts of human complexities since. This is a book your child will spend hours with and learn much from.

Pretzel by Margaret Rey, Scholastic, 1944. My twenty-nine-year-old daughter Jasmine's favorite love story—the tale of a

Story Power

Books with animal characters—like Russell Hoban's Frances books—can teach important lessons in charming and non-threatening ways. In *A Baby Sister for Frances*, the whimsical badgerette deals with sibling rivalry. In *A Birthday for Frances*, the ebb and tide of generosity and jealousy when it's someone else's birthday. In *Bedtime for Frances*, the fears of going to bed. In *Bread and Jam for Frances*, the parent/child struggle over eating the right foods.

All of these typical childhood problems could be dealt with in a once-removed setting, with a human character like Ira in *Ira Sleeps Over*. But they wouldn't pack the wallop they do with Frances.

That's because these books address something scarier than being lost, poverty, or embarrassment. They address the child's fear of his own emotions.

Though sibling rivalry and anger toward parents are normal, the child doesn't know that—and when these feelings well up, they're ugly and frightening. *Mommy says I'm good when I'm nice to the baby. But when he cries I want to smoosh the pillow over his face. I must be very bad.*

Unlike adults, who can reason through emotional conflicts, children lack the language and tools. What works for them are stories twice-removed, where the unreasonable feelings are projected onto a creature that looks different on the outside but seems much the same inside. That Frances is transparent, that she warbles funny tunes about her quandaries, and that her parents love her no matter what—these make the stories even more appealing and fill the child with hope.

prize-winning dachshund who can't win the heart of the lady dachshund across the street. Unimpressed by the physical qualities that others admire, she finally is able to give her heart when she sees his capacity to sacrifice for others. Marriage and family are the ultimate prize in this old-fashioned, heartwarming story.

And for the child who's gone beyond emotional rumbles and spun into out-of-control, for anyone who ever had a tantrum and didn't know how to stop, there's *Where the Wild Things Are*.

Though some Christians shun this book—following the lead of one critic who claimed it celebrates "unfettered rebellion"—they're missing a really special and reassuring message for their children. Here's the real scoop:

Max misbehaves at dinner and is sent to his room (Max has parents who care enough to punish him when necessary).

Max sails away to an island full of Wild Things (Max cranks up his tantrum—a "wild rumpus" with the Wild Things).

Max, "King of All the Wild Things," finally commands them to stop (he realizes he's in charge and takes control of his emotions).

Though the Wild Things beg him to stay, Max sails home again (he makes the right decision).

In his room, he finds his dinner—still warm—waiting (he regains stability, and his parents haven't stopped loving him).

Who hasn't been where the wild things are, giving in to an emotional outburst and then having to regroup? *Enough's enough!*—that's what I hear Max saying, and I see his story teaching children to say that as well. All without a word of preaching or a wag of a finger.

So use discernment—there's more to stories than meets the eye.

Read-N-Grow Picture Bible by Word Books, 1979. Two thousand pictures (six per page, with a sentence or two under each) will take your child through the Bible from start to finish. My children have loved this motivational format, which has really reinforced the historical continuity of the Bible.

St. Jerome and the Lion by Margaret Hodges, Orchard Books, 1991. Jerome, the medieval monk who lived in Bethlehem and translated the Bible into Latin, earns the devotion of a lion by removing a thorn from his paw. When the monastery's donkey is stolen, the other monks accuse the lion of having eaten it, but only Jerome refuses to condemn him, and is proven right.

The Story about Ping by Marjorie Flack, Viking Press, 1933. A lilting and funny story about a little duck who lives with his comically large family on a boat on the Yangtze River in China. One day while searching for food, he finds himself left behind. Bravely, he goes in search of his family, finding many adventures along the way.

The Story of Babar by Jean De Brunhoff, Random House, 1931. This book, originally written in French, has delighted children and adults for decades. The story of an elephant who loses his mother to hunters, wanders to the city, buys a new wardrobe, becomes the hit of society, marries Celeste, and is crowned King of the Elephants.

The Story of Ferdinand by Munro Leaf, Scholastic, 1936. One of the best-selling children's books of all time, this story is about a peaceful bull who would rather sit beneath a tree smelling flowers than fight in the bull ring.

William Tell by Margaret Early, Harry N. Abrams, 1991. A story of courage and purpose. The fourteenth-century Swiss folk hero is forced to shoot an apple from his son's head by the evil governor, then leads his countrymen into action against Austria's tyranny. Still a man who thinks of himself more as a husband and father than a hero.

The Year at Maple Hill Farm by Alice and Martin Provensen, Aladdin, 1978. A year in the country with all its seasonal changes—the work, play, and rewards of life on a farm.

Movies: Snuggle-Up Videos

I remember in 1985 when Tripp came home and told me there was a machine we could buy that made it possible to see old movies anytime we wanted. It was New Year's Eve; we rushed to the store

Reading Aloud

Just because your child is reading solo, don't stop reading aloud. And though you are careful to make sure that the books he reads himself are at his reading level, your own reading to your child can be well above—in fact, it can be at yours.

For eighteen years my husband, Tripp, has read nightly to our children, including many classics (*Treasure Island, David Copperfield*) and works as sophisticated as the Lord of the Rings trilogy. In listening to stories, your child does not have to understand every word. He will absorb the richness of the language and a lot of meaning simply through context and the drama with which you read.

In addition, this early experience of listening to a grown-up read grown-up literature establishes a pattern of how the child will read when he reads to himself. If he has first heard the classics read with enthusiasm and emotion, he will bring these qualities to his own reading later on.

His comprehension will be better also. A child who has spent a lot of time concentrating and listening will find it easy to read without distraction from within or without. He'll be able to get the most from all forms of entertainment later on.

Perhaps most of all, he will bring to his reading experience all the warmth and good feeling that is his through the special moments he has shared with the people most important to him in all the world—his parents.

Tripp's nightly reading has not only built a special bond between him and the children but also between our children and good literature. Our family life has been greatly enriched by the cozy hours he has spent.

Think of this: in twenty years no one will remember whether you finished cleaning up before you went to bed each night. Neither will they remember if you solved that programming problem or landed that important customer. But your children will always remember the books you read, the talks you had, and the lessons they learned at your knee.

Both Tripp and I can say with assurance that you will look back on the times you have spent reading to your children as some of the best-spent hours of your life.

Twenty Ways to Encourage Reading

Visit the library. Then read books together with a picnic lunch on a blanket somewhere special.

Invest in books. Look for lightly used books at garage sales. Buy inexpensive paperbacks from discount stores.

Care for books. Teach children to handle books as though they had great value. They do.

Create a reading nook. Fill a cozy spot with pillows, hang a few small pictures of people reading.

Turn down the volume. Create a quieter atmosphere at home—less TV, radio, and other distractions.

Give books as gifts. Ask Grandma too! Books are gifts that never stop giving.

Subscribe to magazines. Your kids will look forward each month to their own. Focus on the Family has great age-appropriate magazines: *Clubhouse Jr.*, *Clubhouse*, *Breakaway* (teen boys), *Brio* (teen girls).

Pursue special interests through books. A reluctant reader/baseball nut may like reading books on baseball heroes. There are books on every interest under the sun.

Listen to audiocassettes. To break the TV habit, build a bridge with audiocassettes—books on tape or the Focus on the Family Radio Theater or the Odyssey series. Without visual cues, children learn to exercise imagination.

Introduce series books. Following one or two main characters—like the Hardy Boys—can build a reading habit in an on again/off again reader.

he'd heard about and bought a monitor (we didn't own a TV) and a VCR. We rented *West Side Story* and *Some Like It Hot.*

For two movie buffs whose dating days were pretty much over with four kids and a fifth one on the way, and who had dumped TV to keep our kids from soaking up sitcom sarcasm and sexual innuendo (and this back in the days of just four channels!), videos were a godsend. Who needed to go out, when for less

Watch movies of classics. Watch *Little Women, A Tale of Two Cities,* or *The Man in the Iron Mask*—then give the book to your child to read (abridged versions for younger readers).

Visit bookstores. Many bookstores are very child-friendly, with inviting sections for children.

Attend a book signing. Check local bookstores for upcoming readings by children's authors. Buy a copy and get it autographed.

Tolerate comic books. As long as they're decent, comic books are okay to encourage kids who might not otherwise read. My kids loved the TinTin books, which are translated from French and have pages of cartoon panels.

Publish your child's book. Help your child write and illustrate his own book. Show how to make a cover and cover page, with author, date, and city. Print on the computer and distribute copies to friends and family.

Give a diary. Teach your child how to journal, including reading back over what she has written.

Set the pace. As your child takes on longer books, review them with him first for total pages then set a daily goal and target date to finish.

Read aloud. No child is too old to be read to. Choose a rich book like *David Copperfield*—it's most stimulating to read several notches above your child's own reading level.

Read together. Take turns reading—plays and skits are great fun for families.

Read yourself. You are your child's true hero. Make reading a priority, and your kids most likely will too!

than the cost of a haircut we could keep our family entertained for hours? Add to that how videos increased our parental teaching power—an unbeatable way to broaden children's horizons, showing how people live in other families, other regions, other cultures, and other times. Videos made it possible to bring the world into our living room.

No doubt about it, movies do so much more than entertain. They also shape the way we think. As Paul Harvey has written, "Nobody could have persuaded a generation of Americans to produce a baby boom, but Shirley Temple movies made every couple want to have one. Military enlistments for our Air Force were lagging until almost overnight a movie called *Top Gun* had recruits standing in line."

Not only do I agree with Mr. Harvey, I'll take it a step farther: movies we watch at home with our children, in a more immediate and intimate setting, have several times the impact. Savvy parents can teach so much with so little effort just by choosing wisely what their children watch. There are, certainly, the good, the bad, and the downright horrible when it comes to movies. It can make the local video store seem like a field of land mines. Murder here, mayhem there, coarseness and sick humor everywhere—so much to avoid while digging for the gems sparkling quietly in between.

Just keep digging. And check out these I know will make your trip worthwhile—thirty-four cinematic treasures our family has enjoyed viewing and discussing again and again. I call them "Snuggle-Up Videos."

Top Ten Family-Friendly Videos

Never underestimate the power of stories. Though a hero may be a dog or an ant or a toy cowboy, their trials and triumphs may illustrate heroic themes. In fact, with young children—who are not yet developmentally ready to understand abstract concepts—this is the most effective way to teach values. Before writing off a movie because it has a villain or two, consider how the Bible presents good guys and bad guys. The portrayal of evil serves a rich purpose in the development of the child's sense of security, as long as good clearly triumphs and right is done in the end.

The following films touch hearts, soothe unspoken fears, and resonate with a child's need to know that even the smallest is important.

Ten Cuddle-Up Family Films

101 Dalmatians (1961, Disney, G)—A standout among Disney animation for spotlighting loving marriages and strong family bonds. Reassuring themes; there is always plenty of parental love to go around, there are family friends who care and will help, and good is smarter than evil.

Balto (1995, Universal, G)—Based on a true story, this movie tells of an Alaskan dog who faces rejection and contempt because of his heritage (half wolf), but when help is desperately needed succeeds where others have failed. His bravery saves lives and brings him recognition as a hero forever.

A Bug's Life (1998, Buena Vista, G)—An ant can't seem to do anything right. What's worse, he just doesn't seem like all the others. But when his colony is threatened, he rises above his feelings of inferiority, outwits the enemy, and saves his friends.

Charlotte's Web (1973, Paramount, G)—E. B. White's tale of a motley group of barnyard animals who rally together to save a pig from the dinner table. Charlotte is a clever spider who uses her gifts to save the life of a friend, then loses her own. A safe structure for learning about loss.

Children of Paradise (Miramax, 1999, PG)—Subtitled Iranian gem about a boy who chooses not to trouble his already overburdened parents with the news that he has lost his sister's only pair of shoes. After weeks of sharing his own shoes, he seizes the opportunity to win a new pair for her—a work of hope and sacrifice and love.

The Man from Snowy River (1982, Twentieth Century Fox, PG)—A young Australian loses his father and must find his own way in the world. Against breathtaking scenery and heart-pounding horse scenes (a little intense for young children, so snuggle them during these parts), the young man proves those who doubt him wrong.

Pollyanna (1960, Disney, G)—After the death of her missionary father and mother, a young girl comes to live with her domineering aunt in a town awash in negativity. Her joy and optimism win out over all and succeed in transforming the town.

The Sound of Music (1965, CBS, G)—A young nun rises to the occasion when asked to care for seven children whose mother has died and whose father's heart has grown cold. She teaches them to love and laugh and sing, rekindles their father's heart, and finally finds her true calling as mother of a musical family.

Stuart Little (1999, Columbia/Sony, PG)—A tiny mouse with an enormous heart wins the love of all in his adopted human family. All, that is, except the family cat, who delivers Stuart into danger before a change of heart leads him to undo the wrong he's done. Especially uplifting for the graciousness and good manners of the family, and the happiest of endings.

Toy Story II (1999, Buena Vista, G)—A toy cowboy is stolen by an obsessive collector and reunited with the other toy characters from his old television show. Though Woody is persuaded for a while that being admired forever in a museum will be a better life, he eventually opts to remain loyal and true to the boy who loves him here and now.

But Everyone Else Is Seeing It!

For any parent who's ever taken their kids to an innocent-sounding movie only to be embarrassed by crude language and situations, or for parents not sure about a new movie their kids want to see, here's help:

www.gradingthemovies.com—a comprehensive site for parents that not only grades each movie on violence, sexual content, language, drugs/alcohol, and overall, but also suggests questions for family discussions and suggests alternatives for more family-friendly fare. Click on "The Big Picture" for a helpful analysis of movie violence.

www.screenit.com—extremely detailed plot summaries and listings of every objectionable moment in the movie, as well as rating artistic merit and viewer ratings with demographic breakdown.

Though not specifically Christian, these sites are thorough and unbiased. Three specifically Christian sites helping parents make informed choices are:

www.pluggedinonline.com

www.crosswalk.com

www.movieguide.org

Each of these also analyzes movies for worldview, picking up on anti-Christian bias that neutral sites don't notice.

I never let my kids see a movie unless I've read a couple of reviews from these sites. And just because you approve a movie, don't skip the reviews on the sequel. For instance, *Legally Blonde* was only slightly objectionable, but its sequel had a new director—one with a very pro-homosexual, anti-Christian agenda, which he made no bones about in interviews and which would probably alarm many parents.

Just as in books, many movies have a political or spiritual agenda as a subtext—even in children's animation. Disney's *Pocahontas*, for instance, was crafted around Native American spiritism. An informed mommy can guide her kids either through rejecting movies out of synch with her worldview or—and I prefer this approach—discussing the differences beforehand. "When we see *Pocahontas*, you'll notice the tree seems to come alive and Pocahontas speaks to it. Some people believe that trees have spirits. We love trees because God made them and because they're beautiful and useful. But this is just a story. Trees don't have spirits, and they can't hear us or talk to us."

Don't Shy Away from Subtitles!

As a young mother living in San Francisco and a real movie nut, I seized every opportunity I could to go to the old movie theaters with double features that changed daily, offering lots of old movies and foreign fare. My daughter Jasmine—then three or four—was often my sidekick, as she enjoyed sitting quietly and watching with me.

We'd seen many a movie together when during one she finally piped up, "Mom, they aren't speaking English, are they?"

This actually shows how much children understand just from the body language and facial expressions—all the nonverbal communication—of the characters.

If you've shied away from subtitles, they're not that hard to get used to. And there's good reason to, because there are some foreign films that make great family entertainment.

Today, when our family watches a foreign movie at home, I hold any nonreaders on my lap and whisper the subtitles aloud, but very quietly, for them.

Being able to finally read subtitles gives our newest readers something special to rejoice over too.

Ten Classics Your Kids Will Love

Even today's most techno-savvy kids—accustomed to vibrant color and sound, all the bells and whistles—respond to a story well told. They can handle black and white. And just as we encourage children to read classics, we can encourage them to see them. Like best-loved books, these films with kid-appeal have stood the test of time to become part of our heritage. Filmed during Hollywood's wholesome heyday, most were never rated (NR).

Beauty and the Beast (1946, Lopert Films, NR, French with subtitles)—An enchanting and artful version of the fable of a self-sacrificing young woman who takes her father's place as hostage in the castle of a beast. She overcomes her fear, the beast overcomes his mistrust, and finally her love and compassion release a prince. 7+

Captains Courageous (1937, Warner, NR)—Rudyard Kipling's story of a spoiled rich boy, neglected by his father, who is lost at sea, rescued by a Portuguese fisherman, and made to work hard and behave respectfully. But his heart is not the only one changed, as seen in his reunion with his now-loving father. All ages.

David Copperfield (1935, Warner, NR)—A faithful and viewer-friendly book-to-screen translation, abounding in Christian themes. Among a multitude of fascinating Dickens characters, an unwanted boy endures trials to prove that gentle kindness triumphs over all adversity. 5+

Go West (1940, Warner, NR)—The Marx Brothers go western in this hilarious comedy—not the most popular of their films with adults, but a kids' favorite. Choose this when you're willing to watch something just plain silly. All ages.

Gone with the Wind (1939, Warner, G)—The Civil War becomes compellingly real in this more than three hour epic, best savored snuggled up on a wintry afternoon. The contrast between Scarlett O'Hara—self-centered, willful, and proud—and her loving friend Melanie will spark many a family discussion. 8+

It's a Wonderful Life (1946, Republic, NR)—A man grows bitter at the thwarting of his boyhood dreams of leaving his small town and doing big things. As crises mount, he thinks the world would have been better off without him, until a loveable angel shows him what big things he's really done. All ages.

March of the Wooden Soldiers (1934, Third Coast, NR)—Pass up later versions and choose the Laurel and Hardy version. Santa Claus's assistants make a mistake that ends up saving Toyland from evil in this classic Mother Goose tale set to music and laughter. All ages.

Let It Perk

Some films are pure entertainment—like *The Money Pit* or *North* or *Singin' in the Rain*. Some are just plain silly, like anything Marx Brothers. Laughter is good for the soul.

Then there are films with important themes. Don't think in terms of asking questions even as the credits are rolling. I've found it more beneficial to say good night and wait until the next day to hear what my kids have to say. That gives them a chance to synthesize what they've just seen with things they've learned before, to recall Scriptures that might be relevant, and to hear any wisdom the still, small voice may impart.

The point is, I want my kids to think about the movie and then we'll discuss it, rather than my controlling the outcome of the process.

Seven Samurai (1954, Home Vision, NR, subtitles)—In this Japanese epic, the granddaddy of many American films, a village threatened by marauders hires seven professional soldiers to protect them. Detailed, fascinating, and perceptive look at human nature and relationships. 8+

Singin' in the Rain (1951, Warner, G)—Thoroughly entertaining musical send-up of a pivotal point in Hollywood history—the transition from silent movies to talkies. Gene Kelly and Debbie Reynolds shine, the musical numbers sparkle, and laughs abound. All ages.

The Wizard of Oz (1939, MGM, G)—Dorothy longs to find a place "where troubles melt like lemon drops." Her unexpected journey to Oz is rich in reassurance about the things we often think we have in short supply—brains and hearts and courage—and a long-lasting reminder that there's really "no place like home." All ages, though some little children are very scared of the Wicked Witch.

Ten Must-See Films with Christian Themes

C. S. Lewis, when asked whether he planned the Chronicles of Narnia to be a Christian allegory, said no—he just set out to write a story. The Christian themes bubbled up of their own accord.

The book of Esther records a moment of history that reveals God's plan, purpose, love, and might—all without a mention of his name.

Both of these examples show that a movie doesn't have to be overtly Christian to contain a deeply Christian theme. Keep this in mind as you view the following films for mommies, daddies, and older children—films that span many times and places and reveal faith at work in people's lives.

Ben Hur (1959, MGM/UA, G)—Considered one of the greatest films of all time and winner of eleven Academy Awards, this movie is the story of a Palestinian Jew who is imprisoned by the Romans but released in time to see Christ's crucifixion. His mother and sister are healed at the cross, and he becomes one of the first believers. 7+

Brother Sun, Sister Moon (1973, Paramount, PG)—Directed by Franco Zeferelli with music by Donovan, this is the story of St. Francis of Assisi: his renunciation of a life of wealth and luxury and his decision to live as Christ, helping "the least of these." Vividly contrasts outer religious forms and true spiritual relationship. 6+

Chariots of Fire (1981, Warner, PG)—Eric Liddell's choice of running over ministry caused his sister consternation, but because Eric was true to God's calling for him, the 1924 Olympics would not be the same. With an unforgettable score, this movie tells the story of two exceptional competitors—one running to win, and one running "for the glory of God." Academy Award for Best Film. 7+ (No objectionable material, but the slower pace may not hold younger children's interest.)

Les Miserables (1935, Twentieth Century Fox, NR)—Victor Hugo's story of a redeemed criminal and his relentless pursuer, who believes people cannot change. Exceptionally rich story with themes of mercy, redemption, and grace. 7+

The Mission (1986, Warner, R)—Set in 1750 South America, this film offers more questions than answers: What does it mean to serve God? How does a Christian leader protect his flock?

Notable for an extremely moving redemption scene. Realistic native nudity, a tragic ending, but a rich and rewarding theme. 12+ only.

The Prince of Egypt (1998, Dreamworks, PG)—The story of Moses, in state-of-the-art animation and song, from the baby in the basket through his deliverance of the Hebrews from Egypt. God's burning bush appearance to Moses is awe-inspiring. The high priests' "You're Playing with the Big Boys Now" and Moses's vision of Hebrew history are intense and scary, indicating caution with children under 7.

Sergeant York (1941, Warner, NR)—The true story of a plain, poor, and wayward mountain boy whose destructive course is interrupted by a dramatic conversion to Christ. He becomes a man of courage, character, and conviction—and the most renowned hero of World War I. 7+

Simon Birch (1998, Hollywood Pictures, PG)—A young boy transcends his physical handicaps because of his tenacious belief that God has a plan for his life. A movie that has a lot to say—some unconventional—about faith and hypocrisy and grace. Some objectionable language. 8+

The Spitfire Grill (1996, Castlerock, PG-13)—A newcomer to a spiritually dead New England town, struggling to overcome a painful past, finds some love and healing but also mistrust and harsh judgment. In the end, through her own sacrificial love, the town is redeemed and restored. Some profanity. 12+

Tender Mercies (1983, Republic Studios, PG)—A once-famous country songwriter, whose alcoholism cost him his marriage and his career, meets a widow who's rich in faith. The movie lovingly traces Mac's salvation, water baptism, marriage to Rosa Lee, and trials as a new Christian. 12+

Uniquely Theirs: Films for Boys and Girls

FOR GIRLS

Ever After (1998, Twentieth Century Fox, PG)—This uniquely intelligent Cinderella story eliminates the fairy god-mother and magic, focusing instead on witty dialogue, humor, and surprises to reach the same loving conclusion. Wholesome and rewarding. 7+

A Little Princess (1995, Warner, G)—A rich and pampered little girl is left at boarding school while her father goes to war. When he is reported killed in action, she is reduced to being a maid, terribly mistreated, surprisingly befriended, and finally rescued. All ages.

FOR BOYS

High Noon (1952, Republic, NR)—In this landmark western, townspeople profess admiration for their town marshal but refuse to assist him when he rises to their defense. A study in courage and integrity—the qualities that make a good leader. 7+

October Sky (1999, Universal, PG)—The true story of a coal miner's son whose longing for a brighter future is misunderstood by his father and nurtured by a teacher who introduces him to rocket science. Archetypal father/son issues, real-life family problems, sacrificial giving. 8+

The Arts: A Head Start on the Arts

"I didn't grow up with the arts," my friend Shelley confided over coffee one day. "Now I wish I had. I'd like to give my kids some exposure. I want them to be able to enjoy art and music and to understand them more than I do. But I'm not really sure where to start."

Shelley was asking me for advice, not because of my music or art degree (which I don't have), but because she knows my kids. Maybe she'd noticed one of them da-da-da-da-ing along with Beethoven's Fifth, or rehearsing lines from Shakespeare, or studying a book of French Impressionism. Maybe she was impressed that they seemed comfortable and unembarrassed, as though Mozart was as valid a teen choice today as Three Doors Down.

Shelley's hunch was right. I did have a lot to do with my kids' appreciation of the arts. But she'd probably be surprised to know I started out feeling pretty inadequate, asking the same questions she did.

Then again, looking at my kids, how could she have known I grew up in a home where country music and black velvet paintings were the rule? That my mom was too exhausted from eking out a living to do much more than laundry on the weekend? That as a kid, I thought concerts and museums were only for school field trips? How could she know that as a young mother, I knew I was in a position to change all that for my own kids? And I knew from my Montessori training that the best time to introduce my kids to anything was the early years—when all the windows of opportunity were wide open.

All this by way of saying that it's never too early to turn your kids on to the arts, and it's never too late for you!

Opening Ears to Music

In 1998, Georgia, South Dakota, and Tennessee hospitals began sending parents of newborns home not only with disposable diapers but also with Mozart CDs. In Florida, legislation was introduced requiring government-funded child care centers to play classical music.

These innovations were spurred by studies showing that classical music improves academic performance. Now, just a couple years later, parents and teachers can buy background Bach for study time. And the studies continue. One shows that three- to five-year-olds improve in spatial-temporal reasoning (the basis for engineering and math) after six months of piano lessons.

Above and beyond these fringe benefits, though, classical music is a rich addition to any child's life—and the earlier it's introduced, the better.

At Home

Try a little Mozart in the morning, a little Brahms at night. You'll find that a background of calm classical music will even out the tone at those cranky times of day—like when you're getting dinner ready. And if you've always thought of classical music as something for older folks, you'll be surprised at how even the youngest family members will prick up their ears at the first strains.

If you're not sure where to start, check the music store's children's section for many new classical CDs featuring works that hold the most kid appeal. There are even opera selections bundled especially with children in mind.

An added blessing for believing parents is that some of the most inspired classical works are part of our Christian heritage. Handel's *Messiah*, for example, is a major work consisting solely of prophecies about Jesus and Scriptures from his life, death, and resurrection. Listening to these verses set to rich music and sung by the world's greatest voices can be a powerful reinforcement of your family's faith—especially at Christmas and Easter.

Out and About

Check your local symphony box office for concerts aimed at children—sometimes called Lollipop Concerts. These feature short, compelling works that paint a picture or tell a story, often with commentary to help reveal what to listen for.

Look also for performances by young musicians. And help your children make the most of their symphony experience by an advance trip to the library for books with pictures of the various instruments and tapes that teach how to recognize their sounds. If you know the concert program beforehand, listen to the selections a few times with your kids to familiarize them with the pieces.

And don't forget dance. *The Nutcracker* at Christmas is a wonderful way to introduce your children to classical music. The vivid visual impressions will draw them into the music not just the first time but each time they hear it and remember.

Appreciating and Inspiring Art

If pictures are worth a thousand words to us, they're worth a million to children. Perhaps especially to those with not-yet-extensive vocabularies.

Keep in mind how children's thinking develops. Little ones' minds dwell strictly in the concrete. The capacity to understand abstract concepts develops gradually and is grounded in examples they've encountered earlier. So, for instance, a child does not understand the word *bravery*, but he can see it in a soldier going into battle; he does not understand the word *devotion*, but he can see it in the way a mother looks at a child.

So along with exposure to lots of picture books, little children thrive on exposure to art.

AT HOME

For a child, art education begins quite simply—by seeing art in her own home.

Learning about Art: Recommended Resources

Book Series:

Art for Children by Ernest Raboff, published by Harper Trophy. A series of books, each about a different artist—including Rembrandt, Picasso, Van Gogh, Klee, Chagall, and more—for children four and up. These incomparable books are out of print, but check libraries and used copies (as low as fifty cents!) on amazon.com. Each brings the artist's work down to a level kids (and artistically challenged parents) can grasp.

What Makes a Rembrandt a Rembrandt? and titles for many other artists. A series by the Metropolitan Museum of Art for children nine and up. Available at amazon.com; used copies go for as little as three dollars.

Software

With Open Eyes, a Voyager CD-ROM highlighting two hundred works for the Art Institute of Chicago. Highly interactive, gets children involved up close and personal with more than two hundred works of art—with commentary, placement on timeline and on globe, related works. Order from www. kidsource.com/kidsource/software/openeyes.html.

The Louvre, another Voyager CD-ROM, which takes kids on a tour of the famous French museum, with full-screen images and close-ups. Order from www.bringyourbrain.com/catalog/index.php?cat=Kids.

As a Montessori teacher, I was taught to think of the environment through a child's eyes. Imagine taking a tour of your house on your knees—what surrounds your child at her eye level? Even if you have some interesting art on your walls, it will be years before your child enjoys it.

One easy and inexpensive way to surround your child with art is to collect note cards of famous works, especially those that have a lot of kid-appeal, like Renoir's *Girl with Watering Can* or Winslow Homer's *Snap the Whip*. Buy small, ready-made frames, then group your mini works of art here and there where

"But she's not wearing any clothes!"

If your children are of a certain age, they may display some embarrassment over artistic nudity. Though some Christian parents may decide nudity of any kind is unacceptable, others may want to give their children guidelines to help them distinguish the difference between pornography and art.

With my children, I used the standard of the artist's intent. In classical Greek sculpture, for instance, the artist's primary motivation was interest in and appreciation of the human structure and form. Most familiar classical nudes are neither salacious nor vulgar. They are not manipulative, not intended to arouse lust in the beholder.

On the other hand, pornography is clear in its intention to arouse lust and manipulate the beholder. Pornography—including television commercials that use nudity to sell anything from soap to soda pop—cannot be considered art.

your child is apt to spend time. If you have a reading nook, for example, hang pictures of people reading. By the coat rack, pictures of children playing outdoors.

Now and then, talk about the pictures and ask your child questions: "What are the boys doing? Why are they smiling? Does it look like it will rain?"

There are many exciting resources to expand your child's awareness of art at home (see sidebar on previous page). And if you, like me, find yourself discovering things right along with them—well, that's just all the more fun.

Out and About

If you're not familiar with nearby art museums, now's a good time to get to know them better. If you are familiar, just rethink them through your children's eyes.

When you make plans to visit an art museum together, prepare your child. Explain why you need to wear comfortable, quiet shoes, to use quiet voices, to look and not touch.

Don't plan on seeing the whole museum in one visit, and be sure to take a break for lunch or a snack. Let your child set the pace (unless you need to help her slow down). When she is interested in a particular picture or sculpture, read the label nearby for the title, the artist's name, the date, and the medium. If there's a gift shop, let your child pick out a few postcards of the works she likes. These will be the ones she'll never forget, the first items in her own art collection. And as with music, much Christian heritage is represented in classical art. There's something very gratifying about having your child instantly recognizing the subject matter of a painting straight out of the Bible.

Performing Arts—Drama and Dance

I'll never forget the year five in a row of my kids—Josh, Matt, Ben, Zach, and Sophia—put on *The Wizard of Oz* for our family, their own production from the first idea to the last bow. Our family's big, so it lends itself to encouraging a flair for drama in our kids.

If you have a smaller family but still want to expose your kids to drama or dance, you'll need to seek out opportunities. Check online, the yellow pages, or your newspaper's weekly events pages for children's theater and dance—classes, auditions, or current productions.

If your children like drama, they'll probably enjoy a high school production of *The Sound of Music* as much as a professional version. Likewise a community ballet, opera, or theater production.

Splurge on something new, like tickets to *Riverdance* or *Stomp!* Keep expanding your children's horizons and your own.

Whatever you do, don't underestimate your kids' capacity. I've found children as young as nine to be very receptive to Shakespeare. Even if they don't understand every word, they understand the action and emotions.

Final Thoughts

Most parents know that while almost anyone can learn more than one language, those who feel most comfortable with two languages have been exposed to both from the earliest years. The same principle works in the area of the fine arts. Early exposure, even the most casual, will enrich your children's lives now and as they grow. They'll be comfortable in the arts, and who knows? You may discover God doesn't limit your kids to the same gifts he's given you, and there just may be a budding Picasso or Pavarotti living right under your roof.

6

The Keys to Family Legacy

When Tripp and I became believers, everything about the past was up for grabs. With five children, we knew we didn't have much time to get our act together. We needed to take a good, honest look at where we'd come from and where we were, and then we needed to plan for where our family was headed.

It wasn't as though God had been reaching out only for us. He was interested in the family we were building. Though Tripp and I had been married for four years before committing our lives to Jesus Christ, we knew God was there reaching for us all along.

But let me back up to tell you what I mean.

When Tripp married me in 1983, he became a second father to the two daughters of my hippie days—Samantha Sunshine (then thirteen) and Jasmine Moondance (seven). We'd had a whirlwind courtship and were attracted to each other because we were serious spiritual seekers, though, like many where we lived in northern California, we were looking toward the East for answers. From the beginning, we felt we were soul mates. We chanted and meditated every day. We were generous and did our best to be positive people. We believed in God, but only as a vague, impersonal force.

In our first four years of marriage, we built a successful company, bought a home, and added three sons. We were well respected in our community. Everything was looking great for our family.

Except for one small detail no one else knew—our relationship with each other was steadily deteriorating. Both Tripp and I were oldest children, strong-willed and determined to have our own way. I was also a feminist who wanted to control everything around me. The New Age only affirmed our individual status as center of the universe.

By March 1987, I was ready to end our marriage and raise the children by myself—after all, I'd been a single mother for five years with my girls, and the New Age had only strengthened my belief in myself. But God intervened. On the radio, I heard Dennis and Barbara Rainey talking about a marriage conference coming up in San Francisco called Weekend to Remember. They said it could help heal troubled marriages.

As a last-ditch effort, I signed us up. We argued for two hours on our way to the hotel where the conference was being held—but by some miracle, we didn't turn around.

The first night they discussed the world's plan for marriage and God's plan. While it was easy to see which plan we'd been following, I couldn't imagine switching. Why would I want to? But the next day, I realized that Jesus couldn't be just one of many great spiritual teachers. He had to be God's son. He himself said that the only way to the Father was through him.

There and then, I committed my life to Jesus.

I couldn't stop the tears that began to flow down my cheeks—tears of relief and joy and great gladness. And best of all, when I looked at Tripp, he was crying too. We both knew something profound had happened, but since we were not brought up in church, we really had no idea what exactly it was. There was some talk about the Holy Spirit guiding our lives, and then we were on to more stuff about fixing our marriage.

We went home as different people, really excited about checking out the previously unread copy of the Bible we had tucked away in our extensive spiritual library. In the weeks to come, we threw away all the other books and tapes we'd collected in our spiritual search and told our children it was time to stop the Hindu chants we'd been teaching them.

Eventually we came across the verse in the Bible about being born again, and it hit us what had happened. About the same time, we received a letter from Family Life following up on the card we'd filled out at the end of the conference saying we'd committed our lives to Christ. They suggested we find a church of fellow believers. We did.

And peace descended on our marriage. No, not perfect peace. Tripp and I still have the same personalities, after all. But now we are following God's plan, which involves trusting each other and trusting God enough to submit, one to the other. And I'm no longer fighting for control—which is really quite a relief.

That's my story. Like the old hymn "I Love to Tell the Story"— I often end up writing about it. Here, the point I want to make is this: when Tripp and I became believers, it not only altered the course of our lives but that of our family's for generations to come.

From the beginning of our Christian walk, Tripp and I felt a strong sense of purpose. If we had any doubts about whether it was God's plan for us to be together—after all, we really

> God doesn't have to have a lot to work with in order to do great things in our lives, or in the lives of our children.
>
> Zan Tyler,
> home educator

got married because I got pregnant (well, what would you expect from a couple who didn't know God's plan?)—God had left his fingerprints all over the first years of our marriage with the boys' exceedingly biblical names: Joshua Gabriel, Matthew Raphael, and Benjamin Michael.

So, yes, we had some up close and personal reminders that God did indeed have a plan. And intuitively we knew the plan was much bigger than us. It was as though we'd been part of a historical stream heading blindly who knows where, when suddenly we were diverted in a new direction, filled with purpose and meaning.

Not to sound grandiose or anything. I just think families are important—they're God's way of building his kingdom on earth. And so parenting has to be the most significant work any of us will ever do.

Consider Jonathan Edwards, the great American theologian, who with his wife, Sarah, raised eleven children.

In 1925, Princeton scholar Benjamin B. Warfield charted Edwards's 1,394 known descendents. They included 13 college presidents, 65 college professors, 30 judges, 100 lawyers, 60 physicians, 75 army and navy officers, 100 pastors, 60 authors, 3 United States senators, 80 public servants in other capacities including governors and ministers to foreign countries, and 1 vice president of the United States. Following are the conclusions drawn by Family First (www.familyfirst.net):

The story of Jonathan Edwards is an example of what some sociologists call the "five-generation rule." How a parent raises their child—the love they give, the values they teach, the emotional environment they offer, the education they provide—influences not only their child but the four generations to follow. What [parents] do, in other words, will reach through the next five generations. The example of Jonathan Edwards shows just how rich that legacy can be. But the five-generation rule works both ways. If we fail to work at being good [parents], our neglect can plague generations. Consider the case of Max Jukes, a contemporary of Edwards. As an adult, Jukes had a drinking problem that kept him from holding a steady job. It also kept him from showing much concern for his wife and children. He would disappear sometimes for days and return drunk. He made little time for loving and instructing his children.

Benjamin Warfield has also charted Jukes' descendents. What he found further supports the five-generation rule. Warfield was able to trace 540 of Jukes' ancestors. They offer a stunning contrast to the Edwards' legacy. Of Jukes' known descendents, 310 died as paupers, at least 150 were criminals (including seven murderers), more than 100 were drunkards and half of his female descendents ended up as prostitutes.

Of course, I'd never heard this story when I became a believer. But somehow, I knew immediately and instinctively that my job as a parent was much more important than I'd ever imagined, and that the things I taught my children would echo forward through generations.

That was a powerful incentive to do better.

But first, a look at where we'd come from.

Reflecting on our own histories, years devoted to the counterculture and sexual revolution, I found there wasn't a lot for Tripp and me to be proud of. Looking farther back, I saw that our family trees were marked by divorce (not only our parents but our grandparents), abandonment, alcoholism, and homosexuality. With a few very distant exceptions, there were no committed Christians on either side. And not only had we been brought up with no religion, we'd been brought up in fatherless homes by mothers who didn't care much for morality or spiritual matters at all.

So when people use the expression "saved," I know where they're coming from. We're talking about grabbing a life preserver when you're drowning.

And I knew one thing: I didn't want my kids to end up there. I wanted this to be just the beginning of a whole new legacy for our entire family. Seventeen years later, with Samantha and Jasmine in Christian marriages and with nine grandchildren so far, all twenty-four of us get together every Sunday and celebrate.

Celebrate what? Well, I guess our rich reality, the family culture we share and the legacy we're building—all hung on that one moment when Tripp and Barbara finally heard the truth and made a decision to give their hearts to God and then let God turn their hearts toward home.

Unity: One for All and All for One

What's Sunday like at your house? I know at ours, when we come home from church I can't get the food out fast enough. I've never been able to understand it; while everyone in our family eats breakfast before we leave, church brings out the ravenous in us. And with a dozen or more in that state, our kitchen is a whirl of lunchmeats and leftovers, with Benihana wannabes chopping away at lettuce, tomatoes, and onions while assorted munchkins clamor for something—anything!—to eat.

It was in the midst of this chaos some years ago that my second son, Matt—then maybe fifteen—told me our pastor's son had handed him a putdown on the way to the communion.

"Nice shirt," he'd sneered sarcastically.

Matt was wearing a Hawaiian shirt that day—as usual, a little ahead of the curve, because it wasn't until a year later that

Hawaiian was about the only shirt you could find for guys. But Matt's kind of an individualist, so by the time everyone else was into Hawaiian, he was on to the next thing.

I don't know what bothered me most—the fact that a holy moment had been trampled, the fact that their kid had put my kid down, or the fact that it was the umpteenth time it had happened. Our families had had many conversations about this kind of thing, and nothing ever changed.

Aren't we mommies like she-bears when someone treats one of our kids badly? Don't get me wrong; if my kid had done something wrong, I'd be all over him. But if someone puts down one of my kids for no good reason, watch out!

"Mom, come on, no more family talks, okay?" Matt was saying. And I realized all the slicing and dicing in the kitchen had stopped while everyone waited to see if the volcano was about to erupt.

But I had it under control.

"No more family talks," I agreed. "They're obviously useless. And besides, I've got a better plan."

They say a picture is worth a thousand words, so let me paint this one for you.

Since becoming Christians, our family has attended many different types of churches—from evangelical to Pentecostal to mainstream denominations. We've experienced worship dominated by praise songs or hymns; with bodies swaying/hands waving or stand up/sit down/kneel and pray; churches that pass bread loaves and grape juice cups as well as those that file up and kneel to receive the host and wine; those with monthly communion and weekly communion; with kids separated for Sunday school or with us through the service; in school gyms on folding chairs or in grand churches on pews; with people in everyday wear or dressed in Sunday best.

This church was of the formal variety, loaded with stained-glass windows, dark wood, brass organ pipes, and large spaces overhead that remind one of the greatness of God.

Now enter the Curtis family—Mom, Dad, and many, many kids—each one wearing a different Hawaiian shirt, filing one by one into our usual spot in the second pew.

Okay, I know it may sound silly, but the statement was clear: you can't mess with just one member of the Curtis family without engaging us all.

It was in keeping with our family motto: "One for all, and all for one." Tripp and the boys had decided on that after reading *The Three Musketeers* together when the boys were little.

From the get-go, we wanted to build in our kids a strong sense of loyalty to the family and to one another. Having a motto was one way.

Then there was the ban on putdowns, sarcasm, and name-calling—as I mentioned before—and the emphasis on respect.

Kids will live up to the standards you set for them. So by banning name-calling and certain words and phrases—to this day my kids regard *shut up* or *stupid* as equivalent to actual curse words—our kids grew up to be much more respectful.

It helped that I home-schooled all of them for six years, sending them off to school when the situation seemed right. That meant we did everything together—all our field trips and cultural activities. But I think any family with a strong desire for unity can pull it off.

Family vacations, camping, day-trips to the beach or the zoo or a museum, special movies, playing board games, singing, sports—there are so many ways to build family unity.

When the kids were young, we thought in terms of groups, so all the boys played football, and Sophia was a six-year-old cheerleader. In the spring and summer they were all on swim

A Daily Dose of Family

Want to build family unity while maximizing your children's chances for success? Boost their grades and SAT scores, help them develop good self-esteem and social skills, plus help them avoid cigarettes, drugs, and alcohol?

Just twenty minutes a day is all it takes. You never have to leave home or spend a dime. Yet study after study concludes that one simple practice can make these parental wishes come true. All you have to do is sit down to a family dinner.

These days, that may be easier said than done. Probably why we've seen a 33 percent decrease in the last thirty years in families who say they have dinner together regularly. Think about it. In 1970, while Mom made dinner after school, kids played pretty much on their own: roller skating, impromptu backyard baseball games, Barbie soap operas, or just plain hanging out. Dad came home. Mom called the kids. Voila! The family dinner was served to everyone gathered round the same table.

Today's families are different. Many have two breadwinners or single, working parents. Even in the traditional family like mine, dealing with a heap of homework and a gazillion extracurricular activities adds a crazy spin to the concept of dinner.

Not to mention countless hours of parental behind-the-wheel. So how does a busy family do it? Some suggestions:

Keep dinnertime flexible. On nights Zach has karate we have dinner at 5:00. On nights when Ben has rehearsal we have it at 7:00. I look for a window of opportunity, and if we can't all be home then at least most will be.

Use a Crock-Pot. First thing in the morning, throw in some meat, mushroom soup, and Lipton's onion soup mix—or try spaghetti with defrosted frozen meatballs. These are easy dinners that are ready when you are at the end of the day.

Cut back on computer time to make room for a meal together. During dinner, turn off the TV. Don't answer the phone.

Keep things simple—and warm and welcoming. You can serve common things—tacos, hot dogs, spaghetti—with lighted candles and soft, soothing background music for atmosphere.

The bottom line: kids don't care if the main course is fish sticks and French fries as long as time with you is on the menu.

team. That way we would be in the same place at the same time on Saturday mornings, cheering each other on.

Cultivating the arts with the children built unity—they enjoyed going to see Shakespeare-by-the-Beach, where we could take a blanket and picnic and watch Shakespeare under the stars. When they expressed an interest in theater, we took them to try out for plays. At one time, six of the children were together in a production of *The Sound of Music.* I persuaded Tripp to try out, and he was cast as the butler, understudying Captain von Trapp—which he got to do for one performance. At first Tripp thought he was too busy, but now he looks back on all the happy times spent rehearsing with his children as a priceless memory.

Pray that God would reveal to you special ways to build unity in your family. But also know it's not just the big things but the little everyday things that build unity. Eating meals, cleaning the house, keeping up the yard together—anything you do as a family you can think of as contributing to the spirit of unity in your family. So approach these things with gladness and create happy memories.

We were taken one Sunday by a soft-rock version of "Come, Thou Fount of Every Blessing" played by a visiting group in church. No, not the Curtis Hawaiian Shirt church, but one of the folding-chair variety. We loved the words, so after the post-church feeding frenzy we looked it up and found it was actually a hymn, which we tracked down in our hymnals (we have a dozen old ones, bought when our church replaced them) and sang together for the first time.

Thus we decided it was our family hymn. We memorized it and now sing it together at the close of any hymn-singing we do. Jasmine used it for her wedding, and I imagine the kids who marry from now on will also.

We sing together regularly, pulling out the hymnals and taking turns choosing. Tripp and I watch our kids perform as they sing solo or in groups. One Christmas we got a karaoke player, so the family had another something special to share. Then even the non-singers blossomed.

Daily rituals, things kids can count on happening, are the glue that holds families together, creating a feeling of safety. Children tend to have secret fears, not because they don't want to tell us but because they don't have the words or they don't want to upset the applecart. When parents fight, for instance, children may think it was their fault. Keeping things like teeth brushing and bedtime stories on track provides kids with reassurance and affirmation that all is well.

At meals, we begin with singing: "Praise God, from Whom All Blessings Flow," "Give Thanks with a Grateful Heart," or "We Give Thanks." Then Tripp prays, expressing thanks for any guests and for the meal and "the hands that prepared it" (mine!).

We have a family blessing straight from Scripture (Numbers 6:24–26) that Tripp or I pray over the kids when we say good-bye for a few hours or a few days:

> The Lord bless you
> and keep you;
> the Lord make his face shine upon you,
> and be gracious to you;
> the Lord turn his face toward you,
> and give you peace.

If all this sounds like a lot, remember Tripp and I started our family without a clue or any heritage to speak of. These things have all been brought about in the past fourteen years since we put our trust in the Lord. You can trust him too. Trust him to reveal the special bonds he will use to build your family unity.

Fifteen Fabulous Family Fun Nights

1. **Silhouettes.** On a roll of butcher paper, trace each person's silhouette. Cut and decorate with crayons, markers, yarn, ribbon, etc. Discuss what you like about each other's appearance. Be specific—"I love the way Madeleine's hair curls right under her chin."

2. **Songfest by the Sea** (or nearest lake or river). Find a songbook of old Americana ("My Darling Clementine," "Sweet Betsy from Pike," "Shoo Fly") at the library. Take a light dinner (as simple as bread, cheese, and fruit), then snuggle and sing by sunset or flashlight.

3. **Charades.** Children love charades. A large family can divide into teams, but even a family of three can adapt: each person writes down their song, movie, or book on a slip of paper and passes it to the second family member, who acts it out for the third. After all, it's not the competition but the zaniness that makes charades fun.

4. **Winter Picnic.** Hang a big yellow sun on the ceiling. Spread a checkered tablecloth on the floor. Wear shorts. Serve hot dogs, potato salad, deviled eggs. Plan your summer vacation.

5. **Summer Snow.** Rent a snow cone machine and different flavored syrups. Feel cooler after a snow cone. Make snowballs with the ice and have a snowball fight.

6. **Juggle Mania.** Find a book on juggling at the library or bookstore. Use tennis balls, oranges, scarves, whatever strikes your fancy. Help each other learn to juggle. Talk about how our lives can feel like a juggling act. What happens when something drops?

7. **Card Games.** Play any games your children want. Decide in advance to lose. Delight in the thrill they get when they win.

8. **Family Tree.** Share any information you have about your ancestors with your children. Draw a family tree. As a family, write what you would want your own future descendants to know about you. What are your strongest family values?

9. **Make a Motto.** Ask everyone in advance to be thinking of a Family Motto. On Family Night discuss the possibilities, adopt one, and illustrate it on paper.

10. **Make a Banner of Your Family Motto.**
11. **Face Painting.** Buy a set of face paints from a dance or theatrical supply house. Paint each other's faces. Create a drama using the characters you have become.
12. **Memory Lane.** Fill a large tray with family objects: toothpaste tube, baby bottle, small teddy bear, scissors, pen, watch, etc. Give everyone paper and pencil, then a sixty-second look. Cover the tray and have everyone write down as many objects as they can remember. Why did each family member remember certain things? What will you remember most about your family?
13. **Acrostics.** Gather all your art supplies: markers, glitter glue, stickers. Print names on slips of paper, fold, mix up, and draw. Each family member makes an acrostic for the name drawn, decorating as beautifully as possible.

> **S**punky
> **A**thletic
> **M**y brother
> **U**p Early
> **E**arnest
> **L**oving

Present with a flourish. Applause for each.
14. **Family Academy Awards.** Get out the camcorder for your own night at the Oscars. Examples: Best Performance in a Fit-to-be-Tied Scene to Dad when three-year-old Benjamin brought the garden hose (running) into the house. Best Direction of a Chaotic Crowd scene to big brother Joshua during our last trip to the zoo. Special Lifetime Achievement Award for Never Losing a Child Permanently to Mom, who has a knack for finding anyone.
15. **Moonlight Walk.** Go for a walk in the moonlight. Whisper.

Traditions: Cords That Can't Be Broken

Some people grew up grounded in family traditions. Some didn't. Some couples bring different traditions into their marriage. The bottom line is that every mommy and daddy has the freedom to choose those that seem most meaningful, are the most fun, or work best for their family.

There's the glue of daily rituals, but there's another important part of your family heritage that happens on a regular, if not daily, basis: traditions. These are things children can look forward to. Some are seasonal: mowing lawns, raking leaves, shoveling snow, planting flowers. These can become family rituals if shared by the family and done in a good spirit. Think of the lines to the hymn:

> Bind us together, Lord, bind us together
> with cords that cannot be broken.
> Bind us together, Lord, bind us together,
> bind us together with love.

Celebrating birthdays can be even more special if your family has a tradition of making the birthday boy or girl's favorite meal. That can lead to some sophisticated cookery, as two of our September birthday kids like paella (saffron rice with chicken, sausage, scallops, shrimp, and clams). But it can make things really simple. I remember one year when Matt was four, and we had fish sticks and Top Ramen and a purple cake. Like I said, whatever the birthday boy wants!

What about celebrating a new driver in the family? Our family hasn't gotten around to that one, even though we're on our sixth driver, but I'm thinking that would have been a good place for a tradition!

The Non-Holiday Traditions

Most traditions are tied in with holidays, which we're going to talk about later in this chapter. Here I just wanted to mention a few non-holiday traditions we established in our family.

BREAKFAST WITH DADDY

This one is weekly. Every Saturday morning Tripp gets up early with one of the children—oldest to youngest—and they go out to breakfast. French toast or waffles or whatever they want. It's Daddy. It's one-on-one. It's special.

THE MUD BOWL

This tradition is yearly. We used to live in California, where winter is the rainy season. One of our fields was usually pretty soggy in January, so Josh and his brothers would invite tons of friends for the Super Bowl, watch the first half to get the adrenaline going, and then beat it to the backyard for a game of Mud Bowl—playing football in the mud. Everyone looked forward to it so much that if it hadn't rained, they'd water the field themselves to get the right amount of mud. That's enough to make a mother quake in her boots at the sight of the shirts and jeans and socks afterward!

THE TALK

This is a once-in-a-lifetime tradition. As our children turn thirteen, they go for a one-on-one trip—boys with Dad, girls with Mom—for two days of discussion of what it means to become a man or woman. This includes talking about what's involved in being a good husband or wife, father or mother, and the importance of purity.

Of course, this isn't the first time for "the Talk," as our older children call it—as in, "When are you going to have 'the Talk' with Madeleine? I think she needs it." Unfortunately, in this day and age you have to have the talk at seven or eight to make sure that the first thing your child hears about sex is good and wholesome.

Having grown up without this kind of input from our own parents, Tripp and I knew we needed to come up with a plan. Our plan was pretty simple. It went like this: every car has an owner's manual. You study it to understand how your car is supposed to work and to keep it at its best. That is your main and most trusted source of information about your car.

The Bible is like God's owner's manual for his creation. When we study it and follow the guidelines, we will realize our potential. (This is a little different than the birds and bees, but our boys especially seem to relate to this imagery.)

Sex is part of God's plan for marriage. It's an incredibly wonderful experience that bonds husband and wife together in a special way. So as you grow up, even though your body may send signals that it's ready for sex and even though you may want it, you wait in order to make that moment in your marriage as special as it was meant to be.

God can help you.

The concept of purity we wanted for our children was not a turning away from sex but a turning toward God. It wasn't like "Just Say No to Drugs." Drugs are bad for you, and you should say no to them. It wasn't about saying no but waiting for the right moment—the first night of marriage.

We also go over the practical benefits of purity: studies show that not only do married couples enjoy sex the most, but those who have never had other partners and those who are religious report the highest satisfaction of all. But the concept of purity is more inclusive than just avoiding sex. It means dressing modestly and avoiding vulgarity and coarseness in movies, music, conversation, and friends. It means that if you are with others with different standards, you don't sink down to their level. And you do this not by being self-righteous but by being a presence representing God's light and love.

Purity alone is not enough to make a good, strong marriage. Tripp and I also try to convey to our kids a vision of the integrity and self-sacrifice they'll need to raise up their own families some day. Life isn't always happy and fun. Sometimes it's hard work. Sometimes God asks you to do more than you think you can. Sometimes something happens, like the birth of a child with a handicap, and it will shake the foundations of your marriage, no matter how strong. Will you let it topple or work a little harder?

It's on the birthday trip that we ask our children to commit to God to make purity a priority through their teenage years, and to preserve the special gift God has given them for their future husband or wife. All of our children so far have made that commitment (one broke it, but how that happened and how we handled it is another story). We give them a choice about wearing a promise ring.

Coming home doesn't mean the end of the discussion by any means. My children don't treat sex as a taboo subject but instead as something we can talk about and even kid around about, as when my boys somehow think they'll have great sexual prowess because their own father had a lot of kids.

Funny that a chapter on tradition turned out to have a heavy emphasis on passing on the importance of purity and the sacredness of sex. But then again, maybe it fits perfectly. Tradition has a serious purpose from generation to generation. As Tevye, the beleaguered father in *Fiddler on the Roof*, notes, a family or society bereft of tradition is as shaky as, well, as a fiddler on the roof.

Celebrations: Make a Joyful Noise

Easter

I'll never forget our family's first Christian Easter. With the children snuggled down for the night, Tripp and I dutifully filled five waiting baskets as we had done all the years before. But something seemed to be missing, which was strange because something had really been added—our understanding of the true meaning of Easter, Jesus's death and resurrection.

"Did we forget anything?" I asked as we emptied the last bag of chocolate mini-eggs.

"I've got the same feeling," Tripp said. "I think it's just that we've changed. Church will be the most important part of Easter now."

Looking back, I understand the unsettled feeling we were sharing. Two kids who'd celebrated Easter with baskets and bunnies had grown up with little else to pass on to their own children. Yet since we wanted our faith to be part of our family's daily life—not Sunday only—Tripp and I were always interested in ways to bring the message home.

We needed traditions.

Holiday traditions, especially those children can see, hear, feel, smell, and taste, provide vivid impressions on which parents can build year after year. There are many that will enrich your own family's celebration of what might be more accurately called Resurrection Day. Choose a few from this collection, share their meaning in whatever words your children will understand, and keep the ones you like as part of your family's Easter heritage.

LENT

Lent, that forty-day period before Easter, sets aside for us a season of soul-searching and repentance. The forty days reflect Jesus's withdrawal into the wilderness for his own time of spiritual reflection. Sundays, because they commemorate the resurrection, are not counted.

In the early church, Lent was a special time when new converts were instructed in the faith and prepared for baptism on Easter.

Today, churches that follow a liturgical calendar—annually reliving the major events in Jesus's life—place great emphasis on Lent. Whether your own church makes much or little of these forty days, your family will benefit from preparing in advance to celebrate Jesus's resurrection. Children will cherish Easter more with anticipation sweetening the weeks before.

- **New Life.** Begin early in the year (as soon as your Christmas tree is down!). With your children, plant crocus, daffodil, or hyacinth bulbs in a bowl of sand, covering halfway. Leave in a dark closet for two months, keeping soil moist (a process known as forcing bulbs). When shoots appear, let them bask in the sun. Don't forget to leave one bulb unplanted as a reminder of how they began.

- **Devotions.** Lent can be a time of family focus on the meaning of the Christian life. You may want to commit to a regular pattern of family worship—daily, weekly, or whenever you can. Or you may post Bible verses, especially things Jesus said, on the refrigerator, bathroom mirrors, wherever a busy family is sure to see them. Talk about them at dinner or on the way to school, especially how verses apply to events in our daily lives.

- **Giving Up.** Traditionally, especially in Europe, there were no weddings, no dancing, and no singing during Lent. No flowers or alleluias in churches, either. Some families may find spiritual value in giving up something for Lent—television, sweets, video games—not as a penance but as an outer symbol of giving up selfishness during a time of spiritual reflection.

- **Mite box.** Select a charity that helps those in need. Help your children decorate a box with a slot on top. Display where everyone at home will remember to contribute their change. On Easter, empty the box, count the money together, and put a check in the mail. This custom can be directly related to the preceding one: giving up in order to give.

- **Pretzels.** Bake your own soft pretzels (check your cookbooks, library, or Internet for recipe—or buy the frozen ones). Pretzels originated as early Christian Lenten treats, designed in the form of arms crossed in prayer.

- **Easter Seals.** Support or volunteer for this organization, founded in 1934 as a means to raise funds to help children with disabilities. In the original words, "Easter means Resurrection and New Life, and the rehabilitation of crippled children means new life and activity . . . physically, mentally, spiritually."

- **Jonah.** In Matthew 12:39–41, Jesus points to the story of Jonah as a sign of his own destiny. So this is a great time to review it with your children, discussing the issues of sin, obedience, and God's mercy.

- **Easter in Cyberspace.** Check out www.njwebworks.com/easter/ for many, many Christian Easter links, including history, poetry, drama, and daily meditations.

- **Giving.** While we usually think of Christmas as a time for gift-giving, Easter has a richer heritage. God gave his Son. Jesus gave his life. Find ways to give unconditionally: money to the homeless person on the corner, treats for

How can you make Easter, an event that happened more than two thousand years ago, real to young children, who are not abstract thinkers and need to see to learn?

Experiences like growing seeds or bulbs give a concrete image, providing a bridge into the abstract concept of new life. Also helpful are books with lots of pictures that discuss Jesus's death and resurrection. For preschoolers, go easy on the torturous events leading to the crucifixion, as those details could be too intense and upsetting. Concentrate on the tomb—finding it empty holds a lot of drama for children. For even more excitement, make the story three-dimensional and make an Easter diorama.

1. Using clay or papier mâché, construct a tomb and a stone. Create a scene, as simple or elaborate as you wish, of Jesus's burial site.
2. Look through the toy box for plastic figures to represent Jesus and the guards, or make your own. Wrap Jesus in a shroud (gauze from the medicine cabinet is perfect), and place him in the tomb on Friday.
3. Roll the stone in front of the opening of the tomb, using appropriate vocalizations to show how heavy it is.
4. Now station the guards in front. No one is to touch the stone, although with the children's help, the guards may march back and forth to stretch their legs.
5. On Easter morning the children should find that during the night the stone was rolled away. The guards are lying outside the tomb, the gauzy shroud is inside, but Jesus is gone!
6. Read whichever biblical account fits your children's ages or attention spans—some Gospels have more information than others. Then "discover" the Jesus figure nearby. Now the words have meaning: "He is risen! He is risen indeed!"

those in nursing homes, old clothes to children in another country. Jesus told us clearly, "Whatever you did for one of the least of these brothers of mine, you did for me" (Matt. 25:40).

- **Handel's Messiah.** Invest in a CD or tape and bathe your family in this beautiful classic, clearly composed under divine inspiration—each segment a Bible verse prophesying the birth, life, death, and finally the resurrection of Jesus. (The "Hallelujah Chorus" was a celebration for Easter morning following the Lenten absence of alleluias.)

HOLY WEEK

- **Resurrection Eggs™.** An egg carton filled with a dozen plastic eggs, each containing a symbol of the Holy Week. Accompanied by twelve brief child-friendly lessons. Available from www.familylife.com, or Google for sites that tell you how to make your own.

- **Palm Sunday.** If your church doesn't make much of Palm Sunday, you might consider just once attending one that does. For an in-home celebration, read Matthew 21:1–11 together. If you have a large family or a few friends, you can put together costumes and act out Jesus's arrival in Jerusalem.

- **Seeds.** These tiny pods and grains offer a clear message to children of the power of new life. Rest eggshell halves filled with soil in an egg carton. Plant a marigold, petunia, or grapefruit seed in each (or even grass seed for fastest results). Place in sunny window.

- **Art Museums.** The Passion of Christ is the most-portrayed subject of Western art. If you live in a metropolitan area, a visit to your local art museum may give your family much to ponder.

- **Housecleaning.** Wednesday of Holy Week has been a traditional day in many countries for housecleaning—from the Jewish custom of cleaning before Passover.

- **Passover.** Each year more Christians are drawn to celebrate Passover, the feast commemorating the departure of the Israelites from slavery (Exodus 12). Jesus had come to Jerusalem to celebrate and was actually crucified on Passover Day. He is the fulfillment of this tradition, as our own Passover Lamb. Sheresh Ministries (www.shereshministries.org) offers materials to help any family celebrate the Passover, thus connecting the Old and New Testaments.

- **Foot Washing.** This Maundy Thursday event speaks volumes about Jesus's desire for us to serve. Read John 13. Wrap a towel around your waist, as Jesus did, and wash your children's feet. Your lives might never be the same.

Good Friday

- **Three Hours.** Observe Jesus's crucifixion by reading the biblical account together. Sing old hymns of the crucifixion and the cross: "Were You There When They Crucified My Lord?" "The Old Rugged Cross," "When I Survey the Wondrous Cross." Most Catholic churches offer Stations of the Cross, fourteen plaques circling the interior walls that depict the final hours of Jesus's life. You may want to visit and contemplate these, one by one.

- **Hot Cross Buns.** Traditional Good Friday fare for the family to make and eat together.

Saturday of Holy Week

- **The Jesus Movie.** Watch Campus Crusade's beautifully crafted evangelical movie, scripted only with words from the Gospel of Luke (www.jesusvideo.org).

Easter Sunday

- **Easter Greeting.** Greet each other with the old tradition: "Alleluia, the Lord is risen!" and answer "He is risen indeed!"
- **Sunrise Service.** Attend one offered by a church or climb a hill with your family, worship together, and share a picnic breakfast.
- **Special Music.** Listen together to Sandi Patti's moving "Was It a Morning like This?" Listen again. Discuss how it must have felt to see our risen Lord. Was anyone who saw him ever the same? Jesus said those who believe without having seen are blessed (John 20:29).
- **New Clothes.** New converts were traditionally baptized at Easter, wearing new white garments to symbolize their new life. If your family has new Easter outfits, share with your children where this tradition came from.

Somewhere in the Easter celebration, you may be coloring eggs and visiting relatives. Eggs then can become a subtle way of sharing the Good News with those who really don't understand who Jesus is. Like seeds, eggs are very much a symbol of new life. Traditionally they were also a symbol of Easter joy because they were a forbidden item during Lent. Nowadays, dyed to take to Grandmother's for an annual Easter egg hunt, they can bear all manner of joyful messages.

Share with relatives and friends the traditions you've added and what they mean. And whatever traditions you keep, remember that for believers Easter is a celebration that really never ends.

Thanksgiving

I'd stuffed many a turkey before I really understood Thanksgiving. Oh sure, I knew we were supposed to be thankful, and once

I became a Christian I knew who we were thanking. But it wasn't till I taught my children at home that I got the whole story.

Unfortunately, these days that story keeps getting harder to find.

For years, public schools have left God out of Thanksgiving, teaching instead that the Pilgrims gave a party to thank the Native Americans or Mother Earth. Even more current are claims that the first Thanksgiving was a copy of European harvest festivals or a stolen Native American custom or just a repeat of thanksgivings by other explorers.

But the Pilgrims' own writings and the historical events leading to the first Thanksgiving show the traditional accounts (available in pre-1960 books and encyclopedias) to be authentic. Thanksgiving was not an isolated event or an imitation but a uniquely inspired Christian celebration—the culmination of a long journey of faith in which the Pilgrims had relied on God and trusted him through many adversities.

If the story is not to be forgotten, it is today's Christian parents who must pass it on. This year, make sure your celebration of Thanksgiving includes this portrait of God's hand in history bringing people together to accomplish specific purposes—as well as the lesson of 1 Thessalonians 5:16–18: "Be joyful always; pray continually; give thanks in all circumstances."

Tell the Tale

In the early 1600s the Wampanoag (Wam-pa-NO-ag) Indians covered the coast of what we now call New England. They raised crops, living close to the ocean in summer for seafood, moving inland in winter to set up hunting camps. Their encounters with Europeans over the years were mostly friendly.

One exception: in 1614 Captain Thomas Hunt captured several Wampanoag, along with a Patuxet named Squanto, to be

Make a Thanksgiving Box

Jeanne Zornes shares this tradition: each November 1, she covers a Kleenex box with fall fabric, reinforcing the opening with trim, then plumps it in the center of the table with note paper and pen. Through the month family members write notes about what they are thankful for. On Thanksgiving night while eating the pies, the family reads the notes aloud, sharing events ranging from deaths in the family to having braces finally removed to playing in the first snow.

sold into slavery in Spain. A Spanish monk purchased Squanto's freedom, taught him English, and introduced him to Jesus Christ. In 1619 Squanto returned to his native land, only to find his tribe wiped out by an epidemic. Thereafter he made his home with the Wampanoag.

Meanwhile, in 1608, a British group called the Separatists fled to Leyden, Holland. There they found religious freedom but also poverty, grueling work hours, and a secular culture that threatened to undo the values they had carefully instilled into their children. In 1620, they sold everything and indentured themselves for seven years to finance their journey to America.

On the Mayflower, the Separatists were joined by those seeking the new land for other reasons; these they called the Strangers. The two groups, 102 altogether, were called the Pilgrims.

Their journey lasted nine weeks. In one of those "accidents" that change the course of history, the ship lost its course and landed far north of its destination, at what we now call Cape Cod, Massachusetts. Once outside the territory covered by the King's Charter, the Pilgrims became responsible for their own government, and so they wrote a set of laws called the Mayflower Compact.

On December 21, 1620, they began their new life at the place they named Plymouth.

It was a devastating winter—whipped with wind and sleet and snow. Half the Pilgrims died. Still, the Separatists clung to their faith; not one chose to return to England with the Mayflower that spring.

But spring brought unexpected relief—the help of a noble and generous Christian brother, Squanto. He taught them how to grow corn, use fertilizer, stalk deer, and catch fish. William Bradford, the governor of Plymouth, wrote of Squanto that he was "a special instrument sent of God for good beyond our expectations."

And so their first harvest was good. Governor Bradford proclaimed a day of thanksgiving to God, and the Pilgrims invited their Indian friends. Chief Massasoit and ninety members of his tribe came, along with Squanto, bearing venison and wild turkeys for all to share. Together, in harmony, the Pilgrims and the Indians feasted, played games, ran races, and showed their prowess with bow and arrow and musket.

How thankful were the Pilgrims? The first Thanksgiving took three whole days!

READ THE STORY

Pass along the whole story for generations with any of these wonderful books.

- *Pilgrim Boy* by Matilda Nordtvedt, A Beka Books, 114 pages, ages 7–12 (877-223-5226, order #56480). Life in Leyden, the Mayflower passage, first-year hardships, and the first Thanksgiving feast—from the point of view of a young boy. Sparkling dialogue and expressive feelings make this a wonderfully readable, historically rich, and faith-filled account.

- *Voyage to Freedom* by David Gay, Banner of Truth Trust, 149 pages, ages 9–12 (ISBN 0851513840). A historical narrative of the Atlantic Crossing, through the eyes of one family. Their encounters with the actual historical figures provide a satisfying, adventuresome view of the Mayflower voyage, from their first steps aboard to their first steps on Plymouth.

- *Squanto and the Miracle of Thanksgiving* by Eric Metaxas, Tommy Nelson, 32 pages, ages 4–8 (ISBN 0849958644). Among many wonderful books about Squanto, this one stands out, showing clearly that the primary player in the Thanksgiving story was not a Native American or Pilgrim but God.

- *The Light and the Glory for Children* by Peter Marshall and David Manuel, Revell, 174 pages, ages 9–12 (ISBN 0800754484). A simplified version of the adult original, this thoughtful text details God's plan for America revealed in its history from Christopher Columbus through George Washington. Questions at the end of each chapter for family discussion.

- *Sarah Morton's Day: A Day in the Life of a Pilgrim Girl* and *Samuel Eaton's Day: A Day in the Life of a Pilgrim Boy*, also *Tapenum's Day: A Wampanoag Indian Boy in Pilgrim Times*—all by Kate Waters, Scholastic Incorporated, 32 pages, ages 4–8 (ISBN 0590474006, 0590480537, 0590202375). Authentically designed photos follow each child through a typical day, with a first-person narrative describing daily activities and family life, as well as hopes and fears.

- *Three Young Pilgrims* by Cheryl Harness, Alladin Paperbacks, 40 pages, ages 4–8 (ISBN 0689802080). Richly detailed, engaging illustrations of the Mayflower voyage, the first wedding at Plymouth, the Indians, the harvest. Language-rich, child-friendly format.

CRAFT A FAMILY BANNER

You'll need:

- a large poster board turkey (Target or Hallmark)
- bowls of dried beans, peas, corn, and wild rice
- small glue containers

You might want to work on this project only when every member of the family is there—including Daddy. The object is to accent the lines of the turkey with lines of dried beans. Use Elmer's glue generously—it will dry clear and your beans will be secure year after year. Try not to control the final results—they're not as important as the process.

This project will probably occupy several one-hour sessions—an excellent time to share the story of the Pilgrims, and to talk about your own family's trials and faith in God. If you have little ones, work on a piece of plywood or cardboard so you can put everything away between sessions.

When complete, mount your turkey mosaic with glue to a large piece of felt hemmed at the top for display as a banner. Use contrasting felt to spell across the top and bottom: Thanksgiving in Our Hearts.

We made ours long ago when the children were little, and we bring it out and hang it every Thanksgiving. Even with a bean missing here and there, it is a part of the Curtis heritage!

LISTEN TO OTHER STORYTELLERS

Audiobooks can bring a family together as they cuddle up and listen, and this audiobook of the Thanksgiving story is one of the best: *The Legend of Squanto* by Paul McCusker, Focus on the Family Radio Theater, 2 CDs or audiocassettes (www.family.

Five Kernels of Corn

The year following the first Thanksgiving brought greater hardship than the first. During the Starving Time, according to tradition, the Pilgrims had a daily ration of only five kernels of corn apiece. Still, they did not give in to bitterness but trusted their Lord.

Many families now practice this tradition: beside each place at the Thanksgiving table place five kernels of dried corn. During the meal, pass a special cup to each member of the family. Each person drops a kernel into the cup while sharing something for which he is grateful.

Our family loves this tradition, as even the youngest can participate!

org/resources). A Focus on the Family review says: "More than a story about an honest man who triumphed over tragedy. It is also a tribute to forgiveness, integrity and the ability to look beyond the color of a man's skin."

Sing It

Traditional Thanksgiving hymns to teach your family:

"Come, Ye Thankful People Come"
"Now Thank We All Our God"
"We Gather Together"
"We Plow the Seeds and Scatter"

Hear the tunes and find all the verses of these and other Thanksgiving hymns at www.cyberhymnal.org.

Thanksgiving Every Day

The first Thanksgiving was a joyful celebration but so much more. For though the Pilgrims had much to be thankful for—the shelters they had built, the successful harvest, their good relations with the Native Americans—all were still grieving the loss of fathers, mothers, brothers, sisters.

So it's about more than giving thanks. It's about giving thanks in all circumstances, a uniquely Christian concept. Perhaps the Pilgrims were thinking of Nehemiah 8:10: "This day is sacred to our Lord. Do not grieve, for the joy of the LORD is your strength."

The Pilgrims' lives—their courage, perseverance, and joy— show them to be not just hearers of the Word but doers as well. Remembering each Thanksgiving how they chose to celebrate God's goodness and continue to trust him with their own lives challenges us to do the same each day.

Christmas

"Remember the year Mom was too pregnant to make Christmas dinner?" I picture my kids in twenty years chuckling as they celebrate their own family feasts, whatever they turn out to be.

I hope they'll laugh as they remember that particular Christmas—the one that brought me face-to-face with my "picture perfect" holiday expectations, forcing me to rethink and let go of a lot of "shoulds" and "musts" and "have tos."

Most of all, I hope they feel the freedom to play with our own family traditions until they find the variations that feel just right to them.

My moment of truth came in December 1989. Overwhelmingly pregnant with my seventh baby, I was ordered to bed rest shortly after Thanksgiving. "Try to avoid stress," my doctor said. *Hah!* I wanted to holler. *How is a bed-resting megamom supposed to avoid stress? So many people are counting on me to produce a wonderful Christmas!*

Some of the "problems" melted away quickly. With catalogues I could easily shop while flat on my back. Wrapping could be delegated to my husband and the older kids.

Even the festivities were "doable"; I could join in family Christmas carols and direct the tree trimming from a different angle—reclining on the couch.

But the traditional Christmas feast—now how would I ever be able to pull that off?

Tradition weighed heavily on me at that time. Coming from homes where Christmas meant Santa and holiday cheer came from bottles, Tripp and I were just beginning to create memorable and meaningful holiday traditions for our family.

But during the time I spent waiting for Sophia—whose name means "wisdom"—I learned that while some family customs last forever and some change gradually over time, sometimes a set of unusual circumstances can cause a sudden shift. We might see that a certain tradition that worked to preserve the family is now demanding too much work to preserve.

Remembering Christmases past, I realized my warmest memories were not of Christmas dinner, which in many ways seemed an encore of Thanksgiving, another big meal requiring lots of planning and preparation that kept me busy in the kitchen. I always felt like I was missing out while Tripp and the children played with new toys or worked on the newest addition to our Christmas jigsaw puzzle collection.

Instead, my warmest memories come from two very simple meals:

- **Christmas Eve Crab.** Arriving home from the early evening Christmas Eve service, we light a couple dozen candles in the dining room, ladle steaming hot tomato soup into our special Christmas bowls, slice fresh sourdough bread, pile crab pieces on mounds of ice, and melt butter—putting together in a few minutes a meal that's guaranteed to last far longer than the preparation. For those unfamiliar with eating cracked crab, it involves a lot of messiness: prying bits of crab out of the shell, amassing a heap, then dipping it in butter or piling on bread. It also involves spending a lot of time together, creating an atmosphere of leisure drastically different from the hectic pace of the holidays. We do a lot of reminiscing as we pick. And I never leave the table wondering why I spent four times as long preparing the meal as my family spent eating it. Tucking our kids in, kissing their crab-scented faces, Tripp and I feel fulfilled and ready to stuff those stockings.

- **Christmas Brunch.** Our second traditional meal features "Christmas Scramble," a favorite dish I make the night before to pop in the oven Christmas morning halfway through our gift-giving. Just before we eat, we prepare a fruit salad, chopping everything together, the youngest members of the family standing on stools to peel and slice bananas with table knives while the older ones wield the sharper blades.

MAKE IT MEMORABLE

The more senses involved, the more powerful the memory. A beautifully set table with lots of candles and special music provides a feast for the eyes and ears. Using fresh herbs rather than the dried we use for everyday creates the richest taste and smell. The hands-on of cracking crabs or making a fruit salad together are the stuff of which memories are made.

Create an extravagant atmosphere with a centerpiece that suggests abundance—candles surrounded with mounds of evergreens, sprigs of holly, ribbon, and silver ornaments.

MAKE IT UNIQUELY YOURS

Be bold. Don't be afraid to try something new. Oh yes, that was the main thing I learned that Christmas on bed rest. It wasn't the gifts to be exchanged or the food to be served that represented the essence of our family. What mattered was the love and the

235

Christmas Scramble

12 eggs, beaten
1/2 cup flour
1 teaspoon baking powder
½ teaspoon salt
¼ teaspoon pepper
1/2 cup melted butter
1 pound grated Monterey Jack cheese
1 pound bacon, diced, cooked, and drained
2 4-oz. cans diced Ortega green chilies
1 pint small-curd cottage cheese
½ pound sliced mushrooms
fresh chopped parsley

The night before: mix all ingredients together. Pour into buttered 9-by-13 casserole. Christmas morning, bake at 350 for 35 minutes.

Special hint: Make special orange juice for this special Christmas brunch. Combine frozen orange juice, frozen strawberries, and frozen blueberries in blender. Blend till frothy.

excitement, the unity and the sheer pleasure of spending yet another Christmas together.

For that Christmas, when I could delegate the preparation of our two simple yet elegant meals, what mattered most was a mom at peace, who was not anxious or frustrated by her inability to produce the perfect Christmas dinner.

That year, after brunch, I lay on the couch and watched my children enjoy their gifts, read them stories, and rejoiced that I wasn't cooped up in the kitchen.

And that year, we tried something new: Chinese carry-out for Christmas dinner.

And you know what? We liked it so much, we've done it every year since!

Hospitality: Let Your Light So Shine

I'm hoping that mommies reading this book will be encouraged that they can build a happy, wholesome family, a family that radiates health and goodness, a family that attracts others like a magnet.

And then I'm hoping those mommies will open their arms wide and let all who want to be part of the warmth and vitality of their family come in and enjoy.

Even on my hardest days as a mommy, I have to pause and remind myself how wonderful my life really is. All I have to do is flash back to my hardscrabble childhood.

But you know, even the physical hardships would have seemed unimportant if we'd had love and kindness in our home. I know, because I had friends who were poor too, but whose homes felt different. I loved to be at my friend Rhonda's house when her dad came home from work, just in time to sit down for dinner with the family. They made it seem so easy to add an extra place for me, and I basked in the laughter and cheer.

One summer when I was ten my mother shipped me and my brothers off to stay with my Uncle Leo and Aunt Ginger and their eight kids in their three-story house in West Chester, Pennsylvania. I loved being part of a big family.

My aunt and uncle were involved in some community theater, and we went to rehearsals and sat in the back rows. I felt like they were famous.

A few years ago my oldest daughter, Samantha, asked me where I got my love of theater—which has turned out to be a love for many of my kids as well.

Curtis Christmas Traditions

Bringing Home the Tree. We drive to the country to cut our own. Dad cuts it down while we admire him. The kids usually get to ride the tractor bringing it back to the entrance—lots of fun and photo ops!

Christmas Puzzles. We set up a table in the living room to work on the puzzles. It's like a magnet, drawing different groupings of family and guests—lots of peaceful moments and conversation ops!

Christmas Album. Twelve years ago we found *The Family Christmas Book*, a very special keepsake album where we record yearly highlights plus Christmas events, pictures, and that year's Christmas card. Available at www.traditionspress.com. My highest recommendation!

Ornament Collections. Every year I buy an ornament for each of my children—sometimes all the same, sometimes individual. The kids keep their collections in plastic storage boxes marked with their names. When the tree goes up, they unwrap and hang their own ornaments in addition to the family ones, and they wrap them and put them away when the tree comes down. When they marry, they take their box to start their own collection of family ornaments.

Giving. You can reach way, way across the world with your children to provide meaningful gifts for families in need:

A goat to provide milk and cheese	$75
Two rabbits	15
A brood of chickens	120
Digging a well	12,500

The World Vision Christmas catalog contains these and other ideas for Christmas giving, or visit online: http://donate.wvus.org.

But Don't Forget: Family First! The important thing about traditions is that they serve the family's needs, not vice versa. There have been a couple years when time constraints meant we bought our tree from a lot. Or the kids were too busy to put together more than a puzzle or two. If that happens in your family, no big deal. There are always a lot more Christmases to come!

"After all, Grams wasn't really interested, was she?"

And I realized it was that early introduction, bathed in the happiness of that special summer, that made me associate theater with feelings of fulfillment. And that having a large, sprawling family was a fulfillment of a dream that probably began somewhere inside me that summer so long ago.

And that trusting someone to be the father of my children and seeing that fulfilled was due in large part to the time I spent with intact families whose fathers set a fine example of what men were supposed to be.

And so, today when it sometimes seems our house has a revolving door—and there are extras here for supper, for overnights, for weeks at a time—and people say, "How do you do it?" I have to answer, "How could I not do it?"

There are kids whose mothers work and don't have time to cook, kids whose parents are going through difficult times and making life at home difficult for everyone. There are single mothers who seldom get invited with their kids to share a meal with an intact family. There are kids who endure shared custody, bouncing back and forth with no "real" home. There's the boy whose mother's boyfriend committed suicide, leaving her with him and his two half-sisters.

There are so many people like the little girl I used to be who just want to hang out somewhere that feels comfortable and safe. And who knows, maybe time spent with your family will give them something to build a dream on. Ask yourself this as you contemplate this poem by Emily Dickinson, one of my favorites:

> If I can stop one heart from breaking,
> I shall not live in vain;
> If I can ease one life the aching,

Or cool the pain,
Or help one fainting robin
Unto his nest again,
I shall not live in vain.

For many years in California, we had Breakfast Night once a week. Tripp would make pancakes, eggs, sausage, bacon, you name it, and we'd have all the neighborhood kids over. Breakfast Night was famous. Two years after we'd left California, three kids, former neighbors, came to visit for a week. Along with sightseeing, Breakfast Night was definitely on their agenda.

Now in Virginia, it's more likely to be Taco Night, because tacos here are more exotic than in California. Taco Night is a real favorite for the mix of teens and tweens who partake, as is the occasional Deep Fry, which features homemade French fries—maybe because in these health-conscious days it's not just anyone who is brave (or foolish) enough to have a deep fryer.

Any family can think of a specialty or something they do a little differently, and then share it with joy. Perhaps there is an easily overlooked group for whom you could host a party. The birth of our son Jonny gave us the courage to open our home for an annual party for one of the Sunday school classes at our church—adults with special needs, ranging from cerebral palsy to Down syndrome to autism.

On a practical note, I've overcome a lot of what I used to think was necessary for having company. I learned that setting a fancy table or having my house in perfect order is not as important as just providing a place for people to spend time together.

There are so many people who need that kind of welcome.

Tripp and I had a dream. We wanted a Norman Rockwell family, and we did everything we could to build it. No, it's not perfect—and yes, we have moments I'm not proud of. But Tripp and I have kept our expectations high, and then we've tried to share everything we've been given with others.

My kids know they can bring anyone home anytime and they will be welcome. Just put another place at the table, just like those wonderful people did for me so long ago.

Faith: Written in Our Hearts

Every family has a story. Ask God to show you his story, and his perspective on yours. And begin early to share it with your kids. If your background was rough like mine, even if you've made mistakes, don't be afraid to share in ways that reveal the difference God can make in our lives.

This year my son Joshua turned twenty-one. Each year on his birthday, we tell the story of how God used that illegitimate pregnancy to begin building a faithful Christian family—though we didn't find out the truth about God until four years later. We say God used Josh as the cornerstone on which to build a new legacy in the Curtis family.

Your family's cornerstone may have been set many generations ago. And you will have your own stories to tell. Try to learn as much as you can from those in your family who remained faithful through the years. What mistakes did they make and what did they learn? What were their greatest accomplishments in God's eyes? If there are written records, gather copies. If there are not and you are given to writing, begin collecting and writing the stories. Your children need to hear them.

But most important, kids need to hear their own family's story, so learn to tell it emphasizing how God was working out his purposes even when you weren't aware. You might explain how things might have been different had you responded in different ways to life events. Our choices can make us bitter or better.

I've often wondered how two people from the same home can turn out so differently. Not all my siblings fared so well, coming from our background. I recently came across a poem by Ella Wheeler Wilcox (1897), which, though titled "Fate," really emphasizes our personal responsibility in how we deal with the stuff of which our lives are made:

> One ship drives east and another drives west
> With the selfsame winds that blow.
> 'Tis the set of the sails,
> And not the gales,
> That tells us the way to go.
> Like the winds of the sea are the ways of fate;
> As we voyage along through life,
> 'Tis the set of a soul
> That decides its goal,
> And not the calm, or the strife.

When Tripp and I became Christians, it wasn't as though everything became perfect and we never made mistakes. But it was as though our house was built on a solid rock, and though hurricanes might threaten, our house could not be stripped loose.

Jonny, our son with Down syndrome, was born five years later. Did you know that a very high percentage of marriages end in divorce following the birth of a baby with a disability? Now I know why.

It's not that the unexpected event destroys the marriage, but it does expose every crack, every weakness. Then it's up to Mommy and Daddy to watch it crumble or work hard to rebuild and make it stronger.

Knowing how devastating divorce is for children, how could Tripp and I make any choice but to hang in there? I mention this because when something happens that makes you even consider the option of divorce, I pray that you will look back on the story God has already been writing through your marriage and decide to stay to let him finish writing to the end.

All of these things we did to build family unity, create traditions, celebrate holidays—we did them because we wanted to enjoy family life. But they have also enriched and strengthened our relationships and our trust in one another and our hope for a future that will always be about all of us.

Look for family touchstones—events, happy and sad, trials and triumphs that have drawn your family nearer to God and to each other. These are precious and important for us to name and recall to each other again and again. They call to mind the second verse of the beautiful hymn we chose to be our family's song, "Come, Thou Fount of Every Blessing":

> Here I raise mine Ebenezer
> Hither by thy help I'm come
> And I hope by thy good pleasure
> Safely to arrive at home
> Jesus sought me when a stranger
> Wandering from the folds of God
> He to rescue me from danger
> Interposed his precious blood

The word *Ebenezer* refers to something that happened after the Israelites had miraculously overcome the Philistines in battle. "Then Samuel took a stone and set it up between Mizpah and Shen. He named it Ebenezer, saying, 'Thus far has the LORD helped us'" (1 Sam. 7:12).

Ebenezer means "stone of help." Samuel placed the stone as a reminder to the Israelites of what had happened that day. I can imagine in generations to come that parents would point the stone out to their children and tell the story of how God intervened in the lives of his people that day and how Samuel thought to make sure it was remembered.

My family has Ebenezers—the birth of a child with Down syndrome, the time Jonny almost died from pneumonia and God saved him, the time Matt and Josh used CPR to save Jesse from drowning, our cross-country move to bring our children to a better moral climate, times we've run out of money and God has provided.

Since we explained the meaning of Ebenezer, it's no accident that "Come, Thou Fount of Every Blessing" became by unanimous decision our family hymn (don't forget the cyber hymnal to hear the tune or check out all the verses).

Your family has Ebenezers too. If you haven't thought about it in those terms, spend a family evening—I'm picturing winter, with mugs of hot chocolate around the fire, but it could just as well be cooling off with colas on the front porch—maybe learning and discussing the meaning of the hymn, then remembering all the places, objects, or songs that remind you "thus far has the Lord helped us."

And know deep down in your heart that God loves you and will never stop loving and caring for your family.

Roots and Wings—A Second Look

The funny thing about being a mommy—well, not funny, but ironic—is this: while lots of important people in oh-so-many important places conduct lots of important business every day, truly the most important work in the whole world is going on at home, where the CEO is Mommy.

And God is like an equal-opportunity employer, giving every woman in the world—through birth and adoption—this wonderful, unequalled opportunity.

Some may know a little something going into motherhood—especially if they grew up raising younger siblings at home. Some may know nothing at all. Some think they know it all but know nothing (those of us who judged others—"Tch, tch, my child will never act like that!"—are in for some big surprises). But no matter where we start out, we all have plenty to learn.

And that's what's been the most surprising thing about motherhood for me. For where I saw myself as a teacher and a guide, I've discovered I'm always learning right along with my children—so it's not just about them growing and changing, but me as well.

With the birds, it's different. The momma and poppa birds fly to and from the nest many times a day carrying nourishment to help their babies grow. At the end, the babies take wing, and the parents' job is done.

Not so with humans, where relationship and responsibility continues through to the next generation. Then, when your own children finally become parents, if you've raised them to be the kind of people you want to spend time with, you can become friends.

I'll never forget the time Jasmine, in her late teens, was arguing with me about something and her older sister, Samantha, already mother of three, looked across the room at us and said, "Wow, Jasmine, if you could only see. Mom's right, you know—though I couldn't have seen it at your age either."

Jasmine barely paused, but I'll tell you what (yes, I live in Virginia and that's how we talk): hearing that affirmation from my oldest daughter, I felt like I'd just been awarded a Medal of Honor.

Or as though one of my kids had brought in the newspaper and I'd opened it up to see this headline above the fold: Barbara Curtis—Mother of the Year!

So what if that small moment of triumph came a full twenty-seven years after my very first labor pain? The fact is, in the meantime I'd become a less self-centered and demanding and more forgiving and patient person. The fact is, with the lack of outer affirmation, I'd learned over the years to put my trust in God and see my life through his eyes. And the fact is, if the kids had done a lot of growing, I'd done my share too.

Not like the birds, who nest and hatch and feed their young by instinct, only to do the same thing over again with the next batch, completely unchanged. Motherhood is something that writes itself daily in our hearts, as we are transformed—growing in grace and wisdom to become the mommies God wants us to be.

I know it sounds idealistic, but believe me, my idealism is balanced with many years of reality. And if there's one thing you get from this book, I hope it's the certainty that you have the most exciting, challenging, and ultimately rewarding job in the world.

I guess if we got disgruntled enough from lack of appreciation, we could start a Mommy Power movement (the same seeds of discontent that began the feminist movement—only in a direction away from motherhood). We could have bumper stickers that say: If Momma Ain't Happy, Ain't Nobody Happy.

We could sue people who put us down at parties and maybe even get a special mention as a protected minority not to be discriminated against.

But that wouldn't be very mommy-like, would it? Because there's something about mommies that should be soft where others are hard, kind where others are cruel, patient where others can't wait. We may not start out that way at all, but there's absolutely nothing like motherhood to change anything about us that needs to be changed.

At least, that's how it's been on my motherhood journey. I set out to make a home, to grow a family, and to give my children roots and wings.

The most amazing thing is now I have them too.

Acknowledgments

Many people helped prepare the way for this book. My first inspiration to write came ten years ago, and though I've done many kinds of other writing since, my first calling was to unburden, enlighten, and empower mothers—to help you find meaning and inspiration in the work you do each day.

That meant I first had to perfect my craft. Thank God for Dave Talbott and Rachel Williams, who each year bring together the perfect ingredients for writers like me at the Mount Hermon Writers' Conference. Thank God for the people I've learned from there: David Kopp, Robin Jones Gunn, Elaine Wright Colvin, Sally Stuart, Gayle Roper. Some of these good people probably don't even know how God used just one little remark to steer my writing in the direction he intended.

Thank you to Jeanette Thomason, Baker Publishing Group acquisition editor, for believing I could deliver what I promised in *The Mommy Manual* and persuading the powers-that-be to publish it. Thank you to Kristin Kornoelje, project editor, for polishing my work to make it shine.

Thank you to my husband, Tripp, and all my children, who have supported my writing for ten years—even though they see how short I sometimes fall from my own ideals. You are the most wonderful family a woman could ask for. Even as I've done my best to give you roots and wings, I'm grateful you've helped me find my own.

Barbara Curtis is a prolific mother—twelve children, including four boys with Down syndrome (three adopted)—and writer, with several books plus seven hundred articles and columns to her credit. She has received three Amy Writing Awards and the 2004 Congressional Angel in Adoption Award.

Visit Barbara at her website www.barbaracurtis.com or weblog http://megamommy.typepad.com/mommylife/ to say hello or to arrange for speaking engagements.

Barbara lives in Waterford, Virginia, with husband Tripp and a slowly dwindling number of children, as the oldest are growing up and spreading their wings. On the plus side, she enjoys frequent visits by a rapidly growing number of grandchildren.